# It's *NOT* Meant to Be a Secret

*God wants to speak to you!*

PUBLISHING

NEW YORK

# NATHAN A.
# FRENCH

It's *NOT* Meant to Be a Secret – *God wants to speak to you!*

ISBN: 978-1-481867-09-2


Published by Aviva Publishing
Lake Placid, NY
518-523-1320
www.avivapubs.com

Editor: Tyler Tichelaar

Cover Design & Interior Layout: Fusion Creative Works

First Edition

Printed in the United States of America

# Dedication

This book is dedicated to God the Father, my Savior Jesus Christ, and the Holy Spirit—the great three in one—who chose to give birth to this work entrusted to me by that still small voice that has gently beckoned me to "come sit." These words have been a gift to me, and I eagerly share them with you now.

# Acknowledgments

To my wife, Danielle, and daughters for the inspiration and love they bless me with.

To Jim Fisher, whose words, "I think you should write a book" planted a seed that was watered, sprouted, grew, and is now being harvested.

To pastor Miguel Villahemosa, who encouraged me to start journaling.

To Eldon and Judy Blanford for opening their hearts and home to disciple me.

To Ralph King, who by the Lord's prompting, asked me to prophesy over him, thus activating the gift within me.

To pastor Bob Lehman, whose passion for Jesus compelled me to apply the word of God to my life.

To Dr. Mark Toone, my pastor, who has taught me so much about leadership.

To Pastor Ray Jennings, who faithfully mentored me during my early months in ministry.

To Pastor Steve Gates, who mentored me in the ways of church polity and gently nudged me out the gate.

To Patrick Snow, my friend and publishing coach.

To my dad, Gene French, my passionate father who places my interests above his own and who has been an excellent example of Christlikeness through grace and love.

To my mom, Betty French, for believing in me and the validity of God's words spoken to me—enough to start typing and do the initial editing of this book, adding Scripture and the organizational structure. And for cheering me on to be the man God intended me to be.

To my family and friends, who have loved and supported me as I've pursued a life after Christ.

To *The Rock of the Harbor* family, who have joined in the adventure with me.

To you, the reader, who has picked up this book. May you be blessed as you read what was not meant to be a secret.

# *Contents*

# Introduction

If you'd like to know the truth, I am not an author and I've never aspired to write a book. So why are you holding this book, *It's* NOT *Meant to Be a Secret* in your hands right now? My answer, pure and simple, is that the Lord told me to put the words he's been speaking to me in a book and I've been obedient to his request. So here it is! He promised that he would release his glory upon each reader as they read from his words of life found on these pages—words that are not meant to replace those found in the Bible that were written over two thousand years ago. In fact, nothing on these pages contradicts what God has already said but agrees with and strengthens our understanding of the Scriptures. That's why you'll see Scripture texts inserted alongside the spoken words that support what is being said.

And just because the Lord spoke words directly to me does not mean that they are for me alone—some are directed to specific people; some are targeting his Church; and some are spoken generally to the people he has created in his own image for he loves us all and wants to speak to each of us. Some of you may experience Jesus in a new and compelling way because, even with his undeniable intellect, he is still childlike in his joyful expressions of love and encouragement.

I usually had no idea what the Lord would say to me on any given day. It was always intriguing when he announced his subject. Imagine my surprise when he started telling me he'd like me to start a church—an equipping center—and I was supposed to call it The Rock of the Harbor. Now this mission would clearly be a challenge since I'm not a pastor and have had no formal theological training. You may be in professional ministry yourself and no doubt will be amused at some of the Lord's directives. His ways are certainly not our ways—they are past finding out and they are new every morning. To say I haven't been bored for one moment is in itself an understatement!

So, how was I inspired to do what I am now suggesting you do? That is listen to the voice of God? Several men, independent of one another, started sharing with me a startling breakthrough they had in their own lives when they started journaling the results of spending time alone with God. This simple practice was one of the single most life-changing events in their personal development. I had previously felt that sitting quietly before the Lord, giving him my time, was a waste of time—after all, I had a lot to do. Wow, was I ever wrong! Now sitting with him is my lifeline.

Many people mock others who claim to hear God, and for just cause. They might have seen people walking down the street, talking to themselves as if they had lost their grip on reality. Many children are taught to avoid people who hear voices because those people are probably a bit "crazy in the head." The Bible, however, tells us that we are meant to hear God, and if that is so and God does speak today, we could argue that we might be "crazy" not to want to hear him. Jesus said, *"My sheep hear my voice and a stranger's voice they will not follow"* (John 10:4-5). If he is the same yesterday, today, and forever (Hebrews

13:8), that means he does not change, and if he does not change, it is time every one of us begins to learn how to hear him.

This book dives into the details of how you can begin to hear the voice of God with increasing clarity. It will challenge you personally to give God your time and let him begin to speak into your life with his still, small voice so your joy will be full as a result of your growing intimacy with him. You will then find yourself filled with increased faith, hope, and love—believing for the impossible and knowing that nothing is!

When you were in your darkest hour, your heavenly father was there to see you through every challenge, causing you to come out stronger and more capable than before. This book will cheer you on toward your God-given destiny, and as you learn to hear, trust, and obey, God's favor will be released in your life in new and extraordinary ways. It is my prayer that you will accept this challenge to give God your time so he will show you the meaning of Jeremiah 33:3: *"Call to me and I will answer you and show you great and mighty things which you do not know."*

I began to give God more attention as I remembered the Bible verse that says, *"How often I wanted to gather your children together, as a hen gathers her chicks under her wings, but you were not willing"* (Matthew 23:37). I believe that the creator of the universe loves us beyond measure—so much so that he was willing to send his only begotten son to die on a cross to take away our sin, rising up from the dead on the third day to set us free from all guilt and shame, giving us the opportunity for life with Him forever, both here on earth and in paradise beyond.

*"Blessed are those who hunger and thirst for righteousness for they shall be filled"* (Matthew 5:6). This book is full of faith-building stories and

God-breathed inspiration. Reading it will increase your hunger, and you will be rewarded according to your level of that hunger. My prayer for you is that you will be blessed as you begin the great adventure of learning to hear for yourself and come to realize that the possibilities are endless as you give him the greatest compliment of all—your time.

Just as parents show love by giving time to their children, so giving the Lord your time shows him that you love him. My heart goes out to the precious little children as I envision them playing around their parents' feet, trying to get their attention, only to hear something like, "Quiet! I'm on the phone." As children grow older, they become more independent and don't give their parents time because now they are the ones on the phone. If, when we see our young children long for our approval, we would limit our distractions by putting down the phone—then take the time to lean down, look directly into their eyes, and with loving affirmation, listen to their concerns, then they may in later years pay us back with their joy and mutual adoration. The Lord does not want to be ignored. He has much to share with you. Give him your attention and you will find that "It's *NOT* meant to be a secret!"

# Nathan's Story

## (Testimony)

As a young man, I was not walking with the Lord even though I had accepted Him when I was about seven years of age. I was spending most of my time rebelling against almost everything I was taught that was right. I got tired of my dad—a pastor—and the rest of my family telling me what to do. I decided to move from my home in Washington State to the sunny beach-filled state of Florida. While there I did a lot of drugs, had a lot of sex, and burned through a lot of money… but it was never enough. My life was one big, ongoing party. I thought that doing whatever I wanted, whenever I wanted, was real freedom. I was so very wrong! No one stood a chance at telling me what to do because I was far too self-centered and prideful to listen. I got to the point where I was smoking pot just about every day. I experimented with cocaine and ecstasy, and I drank enough alcohol to kill a rhino. The more I gave my life over to sin, the more lost and empty I became.

One day, I woke up in a very strange place—the psych ward of a Florida hospital. As I looked around, everyone was a stranger. When I asked why I was there and how I got there, no one would tell me. I was extremely sad and lonely. Soon a familiar face entered the room—I began to cry as I looked up into the eyes of my father. He said, "Son, do you know what day it is?" I said, "No, Dad, I don't." He said, "It's your birthday! The Devil tried to take your life, but the Lord intervened and I've come to take you home."

I had attempted suicide. The seed had been planted when I watched the film *The Client*. In the beginning of the movie, a high-roller attorney lost all of his money. He drove down an old lonely road and hooked himself up to the exhaust pipe of his car and committed suicide. It looked like such an easy way out. Subconsciously, I began to process suicide as a way out of my messed-up life. I wrote a suicide note, addressed to everyone who cared about me, apologizing for any pain it would cause them. I gathered up a vacuum hose, some big garbage bags, and drove until I found a road like the one in the movie. Then I hooked myself up to the exhaust and inhaled carbon monoxide until I passed out cold.

Seconds from death, my van ran out of gas, stopping the flow of deadly gas to my lungs. It wasn't long before I came to and found myself lying face down on the floor against the melted plastic of the vacuum hose which seared the fingers on my left hand to the bone. My mind was blown and I began to wander aimlessly around on foot until I came to the parking lot of a convenience store. A clerk noticed me, and realizing something was very wrong, called 911. I was picked up and taken to the local hospital where the doctors discovered a life-threatening amount of carbon monoxide in my bloodstream. I was treated and taken to a psych ward—that strange place I mentioned earlier for people who try to harm themselves. The mental diagnosis was schizophrenia, but my parents would not allow the prescribed remedy of drugs for what they knew was a spiritual problem.

My father met me right where I was—all messed up and broken. Seeing his face that day—the sadness and anguish—I will never forget. My earthly father became an extension of my heavenly father. After a week of convalescing, my dad drove me and my van across the country, stopping at hospitals along the way so my blisters could be opened and the infection could be scrubbed away.

Finally, we were home, but I was in excruciating pain for months as I underwent extensive skin grafting and rehabilitation. Skin was taken from my left leg to rebuild my fingers. Doctors and specialists said I would never again be able to drive a car or function normally in society. To make matters worse, I had no short-term memory so I would ask the same questions over and over again, exhausting whoever had the patience to be around me. My medical bills were well over $100,000.00, and the pain of my reality did not end there—but it was a turning point for me. Later, the hospital decided to write off my bill as charity—this kindness reminded me of God's forgiveness.

Repentance literally means, "To turn around or change direction." I had reached brokenness. Like a wild horse, I was no good to my master until I was broken. I began to turn my life back to the Lord. I received all kinds of prayers, and the Lord began healing my mind, rebuilding it with the truth of His Word. I memorized Scripture and a message from Pastor John Hagee titled, "Battle Cry." I now have a new attitude of gratitude!

With the same hand that was burned and wounded, I've written over 100 Christian songs, and today, I am not the same man I was. This experience has refined me like gold under fire. I know I'm still far from pure, but I am allowing the process to continue. There is not a day that goes by that I'm not thankful the Lord allowed this horrible experience into my life. I chose the wrong path and God allowed me to suffer the consequences, but in the end, the Lord has used my brokenness for good. If I had known the difficulties my rebellion would cause, I would have followed Christ and done what was right from the beginning.

Five years later, during the same week as my attempted suicide, Danielle became my wife. What a gift God has given to me. The Lord has blessed us with two amazing daughters. I'm starting to see the rewards of a surrendered life to Christ: Peace—love—joy. Now that's real freedom! I know it's only the beginning of what He wants to do in me, and I also know He wants to do the same for you—replace your rebellion with His peace. Are you willing? My dad always said, "A wise man learns from his own mistakes, and a wiser man learns from the mistakes of others, but a fool from neither." God has placed a special purpose in each one of us, and the good news is that He likes to finish what He starts!

*Note: If you are reading this testimony and you have a son or daughter who has decided to try the delights of sin for a season, pray for him or her. I know my mom and dad never stopped praying for me, even when things seemed hopeless. There IS power in prayer!*

# March 2011

# March 2nd

*I ran a hot bath and said, "What would you like to say to me Lord?"*

## Speak, Come, Go

Speak to those who I set up for you to speak to; add nothing to what I say. When I call you, come; when I send you, go. Spend more time with me alone; I will pour into you everything you need for the journey that lies ahead. Let my peace be your cornerstone. Let my joy be a hammer on the stone walls of the Destroyer.

## Seek Me

Be being[1] filled with my presence (Ephesians 5) and I will pour through you rivers of life reaching a lost, broken, and hurting world. Don't stop at your goal for yourself, press on to my goal for you—it's much bigger. Stop and drink and be filled—then go and fill others for my kingdom is within you. There is no limit to my love; there is no limit to my re-

---

1 "Be being" occurs several times in the Lord's words. It may sound awkward to us today, but the Lord said it this way because in Greek, "be" is a continuous action verb we don't have in English, so the most correct way to translate it is to say, "be being." Think of it as meaning perhaps, "be continually" as in "Be continually filled with my presence."

sources; there is no limit in my perspective—so now seek me and you will find in me every good thing.

## I Will Withhold Nothing

You waver in your mind, but I say, "Be steadfast in what I am preparing to unleash inside you."

> *"Therefore, my beloved brethren, be steadfast, immovable, always abounding in the work of the Lord, knowing that your labor is not in vain in the Lord."* (1 Corinthians 15:58)

I have set aside things for you to do that are specific to the call I have on your life and I will use your weakness.

> *"My grace is sufficient for you, for my strength is made perfect in weakness." Therefore most gladly I will rather boast in my infirmities, that the power of Christ may rest upon me."* (2 Corinthians 12:9)

You are eager, you are hungry, and you will be filled with every good thing. I will withhold nothing from those who diligently seek me.

> *"I love those who love me, and those who seek me diligently will find me."* (Proverbs 8:17)

## You Have Been Equipped

It is my desire that you write; it is my purpose that you sing; it is my plan that you reach out to the lost, hurting, and broken. You have been equipped for the journey you are now on to achieve great things for me. You enter my gates and lack no good thing. Don't shy away from what I am doing; it will bring great satisfaction. Lost, broken, and hurting people will be changed. Every need will be met; every longing for answers will be satisfied.

*"I will seek what was lost and bring back what was driven away, bind up the broken and strengthen what was sick."* (Ezekiel 34:16)

## Know Me More

My peace will be your robe;

My shield is your faith;

My right hand is your weapon.

Your quiet time will reveal me in greater measure.

I want you to know me more.

My thoughts will be your thoughts;

My purpose will be your purpose.

*"For my thoughts are not your thoughts, nor are your ways my ways,"* says the LORD. *For as the heavens are higher than the earth, so are my ways higher than your ways, and my thoughts than your thoughts."* (Isaiah 55:8-9)

I will remove in you everything that you give me to transform—only unshakable things will remain. Like pillars I raise up my purposes to use you—nothing can shake my design. Surrender all that is fleeting; give me what is mine. Withhold nothing from the one who will give you everything. The balance of your life is found in me. The vision for greatness is my idea.

## I Give My Plan in Stages

Very soon I will move you into a new arena. If you knew what I was doing, you would be overwhelmed so I will give it to you in stages. You have only begun to see the supernatural; you are on the ride of your life! Fight sin as you run to me for I become your shelter.

*"I will trust in the shelter of your wings..."* (Psalm 61:4)

When I give you instruction, be ready; when I call on you, set aside your own ambition and allow me to move. Your ministry will be blessed; your nature will be transformed to house my love. Follow me to the ends of the earth and enter the beginning of life as I intended.

## My Voice Is a Gift

You know I love you. To be able to hear clearly my voice is a gift I have given you. I will call your steps in precisely the way I see fit. I will not ask you to do anything that is contrary to my character. Don't let the Enemy distract you from my focus.

## The Horse Is Prepared

I am preparing the horse for you to ride that suits you; it will not tire of carrying you, and you will not need to feed it or give it water. I am birthing the resource. Be ready in your heart; be pure in your mind. The gate is open before you so I ask you to come; step into my presence as you have dared not in the past. Let the path I light up be your guide. Let the signs along the way direct your going. Be not afraid for I am with you. As friends, we will laugh together. The holy laughter is confirmation of the fullness of my presence with you. The breakthroughs are a result of faith.

*"He will yet fill your mouth with laughing, and your lips with rejoicing."* (Job 5:22)

## I Am That I Am That I Am

I am that I am that I am that you follow. Peace be with you, my child, whom I call friend.

*"No longer do I call you servants, for a servant does not know what his master is doing; but I have called you friends, for all things that I heard from my father I have made known to you."* (John 15:15)

Refinement will be the result of your spending more time with me—

Purification is my process;

Redemption is my goal;

Freedom is my cause;

Life is my lesson, and

Peace is my presence.

# March 3rd

**True Value**

*I was watching a Science Fiction movie when I felt prompted to shut it off and spend some time with the Lord. He said:*

I remind you, guard your mind—it leads to your soul.

> *"Be anxious for nothing, but in everything by prayer and supplication, with thanksgiving, let your requests be made known to God; and the peace of God, which surpasses all understanding, will guard your hearts and minds through Christ Jesus."* (Philippians 4:6-7)

Sometimes entertainment value has no value at all. Thank you for the time you are spending with me; it is very valuable to me. It is the greatest compliment you can give me. My presence with you is also a gift. It pleases me that you want to know me better, and what I have yet to show you will be very pleasing to you.

**Imagination**

I will heal the wounds on your soul. I will use your imagination for my purpose. Satan has tried diligently to cause you to sin in order to create more soul problems for you, and he has been trying to alter your imagination in order to keep it from being able to respond to my clear visions. Now that you are committing time with me, I will reveal those open doors and you will be able to shut them one by one, giving no more access to the stranger. When the access is gone, the stranger will no longer be able to sneak in and rob you.

*I pictured a house full of rooms and some rooms had doors that were opened to the outside, enabling a stranger to sneak in and steal.*

## Commune with Me

When you commune with me, I will fill you with my holy presence. I will give you clear direction, and you will know that you are being led. Don't worry about what has not yet happened because what has happened is more important.

Be ready to hear and obey;

Be ready to love unreservedly;

Be ready to fight with the strength I give you.

Boldness is a new beginning;

Doors will open before you;

Peace goes with you;

Praise will surround you like a blanket that you offer to me;

Passion will increase;

Pain will decrease;

Planting will increase; the harvest will be astounding.

Pleasant is this time I sit with you;

Purposeful is everything I say to you;

Deliberate is my message to you;

Understanding is what I give to you;

Mercy is how I'm filling you;

Plentiful is my grace for you;

Always will I love you;

Radical describes how I care for you;

Mission is what I lead you to;

Waiting is what I've done for you;

Planning has been my gift to you; and

Prosperous is what I lead you to.

## I Am Equipping You

Go now and see what I am preparing! Gather the pictures and prepare them like pieces to a puzzle. I will lay them out, one by one. You will enjoy picking them up along the way and figuring out where they fit. When I speak, listen. When I count, it is not one, two, and three—my way is different. I will show you how it is different—be patient.

*"But let patience have its perfect work, that you may be perfect and complete, lacking nothing."* (James 1:4)

All that I am is being revealed to you so follow me as I lead you on this journey, for what I show you is beyond your wildest dreams. There is so much I want to show you and so little time as you know it. When I say to you, "Get ready," I mean posture yourself to receive. I am equipping you.

*Jesus appears to me in the Spirit. He reaches out to hand me these items— one at a time, and he says:*

Here is my Sword;

Here is my Shield;

Here is my Placement;

Here is my Bride;

Here is my Fortress;

Here is my Logos;

Here is my Stenos;

And, here is my Horse—

Now ride like the wind and don't stop before I tell you.

## It Is I

It is I rising up within you; it is I reaching out through you; it is I gathering my chicks like a mother hen.

*"O Jerusalem, Jerusalem, the one who kills the prophets and stones those who are sent to her! How often I wanted to gather your children*

*together, as a hen gathers her chicks under her wings, but you were not willing!"* (Matthew 23:37)

Make no mistake—no fox will spoil my vine. I rise up to take what is mine. I allow for a time, but my moments are calculated. Holy fire will rage against all forms of evil and wicked entertainment will not stand. My house is a holy sanctuary that will be a refuge for all who enter it.

## Blessed Are You

Blessed are you my beloved; blessed are you. Remember all my commands; as your love for me grows so will the ease to follow them. Some do things because they have to; you will do things because you long to. My mind is pure; my heart is holy. Learn from me and allow me to instruct you.

> *"Take my yoke upon you and learn from me, for I am gentle and lowly in heart, and you will find rest for your souls."* (Matthew 11:29)

Follow like the camel and drink deep what I have for you; then release what I give you on my people. Every appointment matters; every chapter is being written. It's just the beginning; let me nourish your body with everything it needs. Let not your mind waver into discouragement for there is nothing to be discouraged about.

> *"For consider Him who endured such hostility from sinners against Himself, lest you become weary and discouraged in your souls."* (Hebrews 12:3)

Believe me when I tell you that when one door shuts, the right one will open, flooding light into the darkest dungeons and setting the captives free!

# March 4th

## Problems vs. Solutions

Problems are your friends. Sit down with them and set the table with solutions—then have a feast!

> *"When all kinds of trials and temptations crowd into your lives my brothers, don't resent them as intruders, but welcome them as friends! Realize that they come to test your faith and to produce in you the quality of endurance."* (James 1:2-4)[1]

# March 5th

**She Is My Gift to You**

*Lord, what would you say about my wife?*

She is precious to me beyond compare. I have watched her grow in faith so much in these last years, and I shout with great joy when she learns to trust me more: another test that she passed, another bar that she jumps, and with swifter precision she grows. You are blessed to have her. She is my gift to you. Her love is so pure; her heart smiles in just knowing that you are close. Not every wife loves her man in this way.

I smile as I watch her move about doing her daily tasks with diligence. She has improved so much in her abilities to mother—driven by a sense of wanting to give her children the very best life she can. I see her thoughts moving in and out like the tide, shifting back and forth. She watches you for balance so she can come in from the passing storms. One day I will give her a stronger ability to laugh at herself when she makes mistakes.

I will continue to adore her as my little princess who prances about looking for approval. She leaps and jumps like a gazelle. When she laughs with her whole being, it is like music to my ears. When she thinks with such simplicity, she shows her childlike faith. She is so beautiful to me. My peace has come to her. I love the time she gives to me. When I release my kingdom, I think of her. I see every victory in her—great and small. This is just the beginning—I'm bringing the harvest and I will spare no expense on this, my dear child. Please listen when I tell you that I will hold nothing back from her. Her voice will become healing rain. I will pour out to those who will hear; she will minister along with you and many will receive the gift of life.

Pleasant is her company;

    Peaceful is her countenance;

        Proper is her stature;

            Lovely is her persona;

                Elegant is her style; and

                    Richness is her reward.

# March 6th

## A New Awareness

When you spend time with me like this, it causes you to enter into a new awareness of my presence. It enhances your perspective in every way and gives you the ability to see things the way I see things. You are learning to discipline yourself so you can be trained in my ways; then you will train others in what I show you.

## I Long for Time with You

I long for time with you much like you long to spend time with your own children. If they were gone from you for a few weeks, you would miss them; if all you could do was talk to them briefly on the phone, you would still miss being around them, just interacting in closeness. It works the same with me, your heavenly Father. I don't want to talk on the phone briefly just when you need something; I want to sit with you and visit often. I love to spend time with my children and to interact and watch them grow.

## I Pour Out Myself

This is a word for my sheep: This is my heart of love; with it I pour out myself on those who will receive. Be not afraid to do what I say for

I know the plans I have made; plans to bless, not to harm; plans to build up, not tear down.

*"For I know the plans I have for you," declares the* LORD, *"plans to prosper you and not to harm you, plans to give you hope and a future. Then you will call on me and come and pray to me, and I will listen to you."* (Jeremiah 29:11-12 NIV)

*"Therefore by their fruits you will know them."* (Matthew 7:20)

In the moments you set aside to spend with me, I will bring breakthrough in every way. No wicked thing will be hidden from my light; it will shine in every area of darkness exposing what hides in the shadows.

*"Therefore judge nothing before the time, until the Lord comes, who will both bring to light the hidden things of darkness and reveal the counsels of the hearts. Then each one's praise will come from God."* (1 Corinthians 4:5)

It is I who purifies;

It is I who redeems;

It is I who delights in this moment you give to me;

I am honored to sit with you in my royal house.

## Do Not Be Deceived

Many will come in my name but do not know me; many will say it is I who guides them, but do not be deceived; you will know them by their fruit.

*"For many will come in my name, saying, 'I am the Christ,' and will deceive many."* (Matthew 24:5)

Therefore **by their fruit**s you will know them.

It would be impossible for an orange tree to produce an apple without me changing its design. Be careful not to be labeled by hidden agendas, but in all things, seek my direction, and I will lead your steps in precisely the right way. You will know my gentle leading; I will never force my way upon you, but I will love you even when you turn from me. When your selflessness reaches out to others for my name's sake, it brings me great satisfaction. I can tell you are enjoying this time with me, and that makes it so much more fun for me. Pick up your sword often and I will sharpen its blade.

*"For the word of God is living and powerful, and sharper than any two-edged sword, piercing even to the division of soul and spirit, and of joints and marrow, and is a discerner of the thoughts and intents of the heart."* (Hebrews 4:12)

Battle always precedes victory, so be on guard and ready to use my sword to fight against the untruths that try to steer you away from me.

## I Love You

I loved you even when you walked far from me—

In your darkest hour I was there loving you.

Even when you were ashamed to know me, I loved you.

Even when you ignored me, I was there loving you.

When you did your worst of deeds, I was there loving you;

No sin can ever separate you from my love.

Even when you walked away—

I was there waiting for you to face me.

And when you did, I smiled and said, "I love you."


Keep me in your forward thoughts and always know that—

I love you more than words could capture;

I love you more than songs could sing;

I love you more than all created things—

I love you so much more.

# March 7th

## I Will Build a Church

I will erect a church, and you will speak and build its numbers; then you will raise up other men to share the pulpit. The plans are made—now just follow my instruction. I need you to continue to spend daily time with me, and I will continue to speak. Keep your faith strong by believing for what has not yet come to pass.

> *"Watch, stand fast in the faith, be brave, be strong."*
> (1 Corinthians 16:13)

Please don't take lightly what I tell you but ponder it day and night. I have unlocked heaven and have handed you the keys.

> *"And I will give you the keys of the kingdom of heaven, and whatever you bind on earth will be bound in heaven, and whatever you loose on earth will be loosed in heaven."* (Matthew 16:19)

Be reminded of this promise when you see a wall that seems like there's no door to walk through. I will light the door when you pray, and it will be clear to see. Now go and stay on track with your daily tasks.

# March 8th

## Peace Is a Reward

Don't prepare yourself for total comfort, but rest in what I provide; then you can carry out my mission with freshness. Peace is a reward for spending time with me.

> *"You will keep him in perfect peace, whose mind is stayed on you, because he trusts in you."* (Isaiah 26:3)

## A Word for My People

KNOW me above all else;

SIT with me before you go into the world;

LOVE me as I first loved you;

PRACTICE doing what I ask of you;

LEARN my ways, and

DUPLICATE them,

For my love is a mighty force tearing down the strongest barrier.

Let the hate you see in this world motivate my love in you. I fill you now so that your roots run deep into the depths of my living water. Be nourished and lack nothing because of what I am preparing. I bring forth in you fruit that can be gathered; it will duplicate itself in my cycle of life. One seed plants one-hundred-year-old trees. One tree drops its fruit to plant many more—some can even be transplanted—and I will use you to do just that. Be aware of what direction I lead you—right or left, slower or faster—it is my way of guiding you.

## A Waste of Time

This time you dedicate to me—some would perceive it as a waste of time, but it is the key to accelerating your destiny. Some won't take the time because they are not convinced—just like you yourself were not convinced, that time out just for me would be time well spent. But I know now that you see its many purposes:

To TRAIN you;

To FILL you;

To BLESS you;

To GUIDE you;

To FOCUS your direction;

To COMFORT you, and

To HONOR me!

## You Have a Friend

What a friend you have in me—one whom you can call on any hour of the night, and I'll be there. When you hear my voice, it will always be consistent with my character. I will never instruct you to do something that is wrong; I will always come to lift you up, never to tear you down. I've seen you on the highest mountain, and I have smiled because I am proud of you, my son. I have seen you in your worst of times, and I was there knowing it would not last. I am so pleased you came back to me, and you stayed in my presence this time. I have sat with you, delighted in you, and wept over you. I know you better than you know yourself for I am your designer—for I am your creator and I am your strong tower.

> *"The name of the LORD is a strong tower; the righteous run to it and are safe."* (Proverbs 18:10)

## Be Bold

Be not afraid to be bold on my behalf. When I give to you understanding, step out for what is right and my force will be upon you, born from love. I will bring great repentance by my Spirit—not by your words. Allow this process of silent reflection.

> *"...and pray on my behalf, that utterance may be given to me in the opening of my mouth, to make known with boldness the mystery of the gospel, for which I am an ambassador in chains; that in proclaiming it I may speak boldly as I ought to speak."* (Ephesians 6:19-20)

## I Will Speak in Many Ways

I will speak to those who have never heard my voice, and they will be forever changed by what I tell them. I hold the keys to the future, unlocking heaven so that heaven will be walked out on earth. I will speak in many ways to many people:

Some will hear me speak through my word, the Bible;

Some will hear me through another;

Some will see their circumstance and hear me loud and clear;

Others will hear my voice like this.

No matter how you hear my voice—I love you;

No matter how I reveal myself to you—I love you;

No matter how unworthy you feel—I love you!

This is my message.

# March 9th

## Peace of Mind

Peace be with you, my son. Do not let the storms around you lead you to fear; rather, focus on me and the promises I have made you, and remember, your wife will look to see whether you are confident in what you believe. Step into my presence often wherever you are and I will bring you peace of mind.

> *"You will keep him in perfect peace, whose mind is stayed on you, because he trusts in you."* (Isaiah 26:3)

I calmly assure you that there is no lack in me; my resources are endless.

## Do Not Doubt

You are so limited in your thinking, but I will reveal a way out every time you look to me. When you focus on what is not happening, you welcome fears of all kinds. But, when you look to me, I show you step-by-step what needs to happen. Pay attention to your attitude and recognize that it has a lot to do with your success. Be expectant for the results I have promised and you will be able to stay in faith. Please don't doubt me in the things I have told you.

*"So Jesus answered and said to them, "Assuredly, I say to you, if you have faith and do not doubt, you will not only do what was done to the fig tree, but also if you say to this mountain, 'Be removed and be cast into the sea,' it will be done."* (Matthew 21:21)

## Depend on Me

People must learn to depend on me; it doesn't come naturally so be compassionate. Please remember that it has taken you a lot of trials and much pain to come to dependence on me. When you face the wall, build a ladder and others will climb up behind you.

# March 11th

## Japan Earthquake

*After the earthquake and tsunami hit Japan, the Lord said:*

My peace is upon you. You wonder why disaster strikes the world. Many lose their lives; many lose everything they possess, torn from their reach while others sit in comfort watching. I am a just God. Rain is set to fall on the just and the unjust. My wrath is also released on the godless systems of the world, but it all works together for good.

Many will realize how fragile life is and turn to me for answers and salvation. Others, driven by my compassion, will reach out in love to lend a hand; some will send financial support; others will give their lives for the cause of restoration.

I allow problems and then offer solutions. Great times of pain bring great opportunities for a new perspective and a shift to dependence on me. Do you not know it is I who put the world together and designed its elements? Why should I stand by and do nothing when evil is so predominant on this earth. I will not be mocked; whatever a man sows, he will also reap.

*"Do not be deceived, God is not mocked; for whatever a man sows, that he will also reap. For he who sows to his flesh will of the flesh reap corruption, but he who sows to the Spirit will of the Spirit reap everlasting life."* (Galatians 6:7-8)

# March 12th

**Isaac**

*Lord: What would you say about my nephew, Isaac?*

Isaac is very special to me. He has such a tender heart like his father. It is one that is very rare in the world: his ability to be selfless, to give to others, even to feel another's pain. This boy's laughter[1] will bring healing to restore those who are hurting and broken, and I will release my faith through his mouth of joy.

Unusual recovery will be observed in the presence of my joy released through Isaac, and you have not even begun to see the miracles that will transpire as a result. Even at a young age, he has my power flowing through him in great measure.

I have also given Isaac an increased measure of discernment to decipher things of the Spirit. He will know what evil is operating and have the ability to call it out. He is shy, but I'm rising up boldness in him, so that when the time is right, he will speak my words of freedom. I delight in the ways he plays with others, unselfish and so loyal. He doesn't want to hurt anyone, so he is careful to share with caution. I smile often as I check on his wellbeing. He is truly a delight to me. I will pour out on him my full measure.

---

1 The name Isaac means "laughter."

# March 17th

## Remember Not the Wrongs

Press on with increased measure. Allow my light to flow through you with a slow and steady absorbing gaze. Remember not the wrongs you have done or those done against you; no monument to past sins will be erected inside my garden. The only perpetual remembrance shall be that of the cross and what I have done to set you free so you can walk in total confidence, not toward yourself but toward me, so you will not stumble.

## Be on Guard

Members of your own house will test you but stand firm. My words will put out fires and will also start them. Let people around you learn at their pace, and don't expect them to understand everything you say. I work through all people differently and in different stages. Keep peace in your heart and be on guard for traps and snares. I love you and you have been equipped to receive my love.

When you encourage others, it is I who works through you;

When you draw a picture, it is I who inspires;

When you walk through the wilderness, it is I who protects you.

Wonderful changes are upon the winding trail before you. The season is changing and the colors will be increasingly vibrant.

## Nourish Your Body

Keep your diet in order and nourish your body with good things. Drink water all through the day to keep your brain sharp. Run in the morning and free your mind to hear even more that I say; this will increase your energy and allow us more time together.

When you are walking—I am there;

When you sleep—I am there;

When you listen—I speak.

Let me lift you when you are weary. Show love to your wife, especially when she's cranky—that's when she needs your touch. Pray for her because I listen and do much of what you ask. You are learning the power of speaking my words, but continue in this and release it to the full. When you feel down, focus on me and I will lift you up.

## Solved Mysteries

I am rewarding your time spent with me—never is it unnoticed; always will I fill you when you come to drink. Wondering leads to solved mysteries. The clues of righteousness are here for the finding; the evidence is substantial. The case is unquestionable for I leave my prints on everything I design. Look closely—look at my pattern. My prints cannot be duplicated, only my intentions.

*I had a vision of his hands outstretched toward me.*

## Give Away the Overflow

Know me more and you will love me more. Press in more until you feel like you can't take it anymore, for it is I who am raising you; it is I who has set your course in motion. You are being filled to overflowing, and in the overflow, those around you will be showered. Don't try to contain it but keep giving it away, for this is my design, flowing constantly like raging rivers yet never changing. You look to me in the quiet and I stand before you shouting love, pouring into the vessel that moves you with power never-failing. Keep me in the forefront of your life knowing my:

Direction,

Perfection,

Conception, and

Redemption.

## Dream Dreams

Don't let your map get muddled. Don't stop shy of the goal, but be renewed in your mind so you will grow with increased clarity. I am like the quiet whisper of a distant ocean—sit with me and hear my voice and I will draw closer and closer. I will breathe life into the dead and heal the broken. I will rise up to the mountains to show you direction. Rest well and I'll speak to you in the morning. Dream dreams and write them down. I will give you their meaning. Be on the watch for what I will show you.

*"And it shall come to pass in the last days, says God, that I will pour out of My Spirit on all flesh; your sons and your daughters shall prophesy, your young men shall see visions, your old men shall dream dreams."* (Acts 2:17)

# March 18th

## Sit with Me

People want to hear my voice, but yet they won't take the time to sit with me. If only they knew my patience. Some will finally sit and will so easily become discouraged, yet my presence is with them. Calming and courteous, I surround each one who comes to me:

Giving away assurance and direction,

   Pulling down strongholds, and

      Pouring out my heavenly blessing.

This surrounding presence is kept a secret, but its benefits are ample and meant to be shared.

## I Am Like a Giant Solid Oak

I am like a giant solid oak planted in fertile soil giving life to each of my branches. My branches go out and bear much fruit, fruit that nourishes and satisfies. Pull from me and enjoy my bounty. You are a branch on my tree bringing forth life. When you drop your fruit, you plant seed in the soil that brings forth the harvest that is plentiful. I water what you plant, and growth is the process I have set in motion. Animals are set to come and eat of the fruit, nibbling away, exposing the seed so it will find its way more easily into the ground, and the fruit is more likely to take root if it is broken.

*"Every branch in me that does not bear fruit He takes away; and every branch that bears fruit He prunes, that it may bear more fruit. Abide in me, and I in you. As the branch cannot bear fruit of itself, unless it abides in the vine, neither can you, unless you abide in Me. I am the vine, you are the branches. He who abides in me, and I in him, bears much fruit; for without me you can do nothing. If anyone does not abide in me, he is cast out as a branch and is withered; and they gather them and throw them into the fire, and they are burned."* (John 15:2-6)

## You Are Like a Branch

If a branch falls from my tree, it is no longer connected to my life source and cannot produce life to sustain itself and will surely die. Stay connected to me; allow the winds and rain and light to play their part in strengthening you and you will grow bigger and stronger in my sight. Let my birds land on you; delight in them because I bring them to you and you are here for them, and they will find life in you as you have found life in me. Provide shade and shelter to those who pass by for there is a purpose for each one. Each tree that is planted becomes a tree of its own and then carries on my purpose.

*"He shall be like a tree planted by the rivers of water that brings forth its fruit in its season, whose leaf also shall not wither; and whatever he does shall prosper."* (Psalm 1:3)

It is the changing seasons and changing conditions that cause you to become stronger.

# March 21st

## A Story of a Prince and Princess

*I worked hard all week and came home Saturday to have dinner with the family. I wanted to go to a gathering at a friend's house afterwards so I ate quickly and asked my wife whether she would like to go with me. She said, "No, but if you could, just bathe the girls and spend a little time with them." I did as she asked but missed a ride and had to drive in myself. At church on Sunday, my wife and I got separated, which led to a big argument, and I could see it was the build-up of her feeling unimportant to me. Later in the day, I built a big fire outside our house and was reminiscing with a few friends. Monday morning, as I reflected on what went wrong over the weekend within our marriage, the Lord gave me a clear vision:*

I was riding up to my castle after a four-day journey, completely unaware of the fact that my princess had worked very hard to throw me a party inside the castle. She had cleaned and prepared food and was now watching me ride in from the distant hills. Just before my horse stepped on the drawbridge, I pulled the reins back and jumped down to party with the peasants gathered there. The peasants represented a lesser priority than my wife and children. I saw the drawbridge, which represented the door to my wife's heart, go up slowly to lock me out.

The longer I stayed outside, the tighter the bridge sealed. The walls were being built higher and they grew thicker. I then knew what needed to be done. I went inside the house to tell my wife of the vision. I wept with remorse as I asked her forgiveness. She too wept and then we hugged and made up. Had this not happened, bitterness, resentment, and isolation would have caused my wife to be a prisoner, locked inside her own walls.

# March 22nd

**Sit with Me**

There is more to do, but sit with me;

There is farther to go, but sit with me;

There are mountains to climb, but sit with me.

I will equip you with everything you need for each journey. No one loves you like I love you; no one sees you the way I see you; you are precious to me. Knowing you are willing to be still before me makes me smile.

**A Vision: You Will Speak to Leaders**

*The Lord appears in a vision and starts handing me implements.*

Here is an increased measure and the equipment you need:

An ice axe,

A rope,

Some safety flares,

Food,

Crampons, and

A compass.

*Then he says:*

I will be with you as you climb the next mountain, for you will speak to religious leaders. I will use you to break down strongholds. It is I—the Lord your God—who will shake the foundation of religious practices that do not agree with my heart of love. Do not be shaken, but be confirmed in the trials, for no weapon formed against you shall prosper.

> *"No weapon formed against you shall prosper, and every tongue which rises against you in judgment you shall condemn. This is the heritage of the servants of the LORD, and their righteousness is from me," says the LORD."* (Isaiah 54:17)

Walk with me and I will point out areas of danger so you will know how to adjust your direction.

- My word is your compass: if you get lost along this journey, look to me and hear my voice, and I will speak to your direction.

- My axe will steady your position and break through the frozen hearts that have grown cold against me.

- The rope I give you represents the Father, Son, and Holy Spirit—three strands woven together to create an unbreakable bond. Hold on tightly to it when you begin to fall back and the rope will keep you on the mountain.

- Anchor yourself to the solid rock and climb with calculated steps—carefully and steadily moving toward the goal.

- Each pin you drive into the rock represents the sin I have taken from you to cause you to be secure in position.

Now climb with confidence and know that I have given you holy strength. I have not caused you to bear any extra weight, but have taken the bulk of your weight upon myself so you are free:

You can walk;

You can climb;

You can run!

My wind moves with you;

My spirit fills you;

My love lifts you.

I have made your footsteps firm;

I have blessed the ground you walk on.

Nothing—I mean nothing—will be made impossible for you because I am upon you—I am one with you.

Commune with me as I sing over you;

Laugh with me as I laugh with you;

Cry with me as I cry with you;

Know me and you see me;

Love me as you seek me;

Harvest my bumper crop!

I will direct you. Enjoy the summit—I have brought it to you!

# March 24th

## Give Me Your Time

Giving me your time is like fertilizing the soil; it prepares the ground to bring forth all sorts of good. Being aware of my presence with you takes training, but the more time you sacrifice to me, the more you will hear. Beware of all the distractions that come to rob this time from you and guard it along with your heart and mind. Allowing your mind to become continually renewed by hearing my voice and reading my word is the very best way to have clarity and visions that lead to breakthroughs of all kinds.

## Bringing Revival to This Land

Peace will flow to you like the rivers of never-ending love lavished upon your thirsty ambitions. Knowing me is to love me; hearing me is blessing you. It pleases me to know you hear; it pleases me to know you receive me. I am filling you again with yet another measure. Your fullness is part of what I prepare to reach out in strength gently to bring revival to this land. I brought you here to Washington for more than just a few reasons: your family—yes; your church—yes; but mostly because of the intensity of the unbelieving, un-churched people in this region.

## Many Have Turned from My Church

Many have turned away from my church and have become lone soldiers, thinking they are a member of my body, although not being connected to it. I ask you: How can a finger live if it is separated from its body? How can a toe still survive if it has no life source? I tell you it will surely die. A church can be any group that gets together on a regular basis for the purpose of worship and the study of my truth. Remember always to include testimonies in your worship service—they bring healing and build faith, which is what I require before a person can join me in my kingdom. It won't take long to impact thousands for my name's sake—it just takes this precious time you are spending with me and reflection, for this is my desire, and as a result, I will surely bring my goals to completion.

## I See Them Drift

You are an instrument in my hand; allow me to use you to the full. People have turned away from my source of life deceived by the lusts of the flesh—namely the pride of life that tells them, "I know better than God; I'll do things my way; I'll come up with my own system; I don't need to be involved in a church to be a Christian." I see them drift farther and farther from my truth and from my institution set up to offer support in every way. Give away everything I have given to you and I will increase you beyond what you have ever hoped. This is what I tell you: do not waver or doubt; just do the next thing I ask and hold onto me tightly and you will not fail.

*"Let us hold fast the confession of our hope without wavering, for he who promised is faithful."* (Hebrews 10:23)

## Dig Deep

Dig deep into the center of my holiness and witness the source of all life. I bring forth the root of plenty so all may profit from my design. Blessed is the one who dares to sit with me. Blessed is the one who allows honest evaluation, for it is I who bring conviction. It is I who give to each a glass full of wisdom so those who drink in my goodness will also be swept away in kindness and love. Selfishness comes to nip at my tender roots like foxes that spoil the vines—beware of those little nips.

> *"Let nothing be done through selfish ambition or conceit, but in lowliness of mind let each esteem others better than himself."* (Philippians 2:3)

## Give Out What I Give to You

I respond to you with full love, grace, and mercy, so take heed that you always extend the same to others. Paradise is a frame of mind; let your picture dwell there inside of it. Constant and assured is my direction for you—don't miss one turn. Your life is blossoming like the flowers in the springtime, colored with a splash of heaven. Dive into me and I will surround you with my living water. You will no longer have need to thirst but will be consumed by satisfaction.

> *"O LORD, the hope of Israel, All who forsake you shall be ashamed. Those who depart from me shall be written in the earth, because they have forsaken the LORD, The fountain of living waters."* (Jeremiah 17:13)

## Complete My Assignments

Complete all I give you to do. If you are uncertain, ask me and I'll show you. A chick breaks from an egg, so I also will break all forms of pride giving birth to new life rooted in humility. Instruct with meekness; be patient, for you yourself were given this grace.

*"Who is wise and understanding among you? Let him show by good conduct that his works are done in the meekness of wisdom."* (James 3:13)

## Pearls Come from Great Pain

Always be willing to listen for the pearls of life come from great pain.

*"Again, the kingdom of heaven is like a merchant seeking beautiful pearls, who, when he had found one pearl of great price, went and sold all that he had and bought it."* (Matthew 13:45-46)

Crack open my wisdom and pour it into your hurting heart.

*"Wisdom is the principal thing; therefore get wisdom. And in all your getting, get understanding. Exalt her, and she will promote you; She will bring you honor, when you embrace her."* (Proverbs 4:7-8)

Bring forth a beautiful bounty of gracious blossoms in peaceful pastures. Travel through my vine while staying close to me; avoid the thorns and thistles while moving toward my plentiful fruit.

*"I am the vine, you are the branches. He who abides in me, and I in him, bears much fruit; for without me you can do nothing."* (John 15:5)

Then taste of it and see whether it does not burst in your mouth with all kinds of explosive flavors. When you look to the sky and see its changing shapes and colors, remember that I have been shaping your heart and mind with the same endless mastery. You are my artistic design and not yet have I finished; there is a time to shape and a time to enjoy that which is finished well. Pull back the hardened layer of your precious fruit and allow others to feast on what I have given you and more life will grow and feed many.

*"For a good tree does not bear bad fruit, nor does a bad tree bear good fruit."* (Luke 6:43)

## Bless Forward

There is an endless supply of my seed, so spread it generously and much will be planted into the lives that are prepared for greatness.

*"Then he took some of the seed of the land and planted it in a fertile field; He placed it by abundant waters and set it like a willow tree."* (Ezekiel 17:5)

Hold on tightly to me but loosely to the things of the world because there will be a day that I will call you from it. It will not miss you nor will it be pained by your leaving, but a celebration beyond what you've imagined happens now in the heavens, and you will join it the moment your work here is finished. You have traveled the desert, escaping with your life. Tired and thirsty, finding safety in my voice, I lead you to water. Now drink deep of me and spare no expense on those I choose to bless forward.

*"Eat, O friends! Drink, yes, drink deeply, O beloved ones!"* (Song of Solomon 5:1)

## Bring Each Thought Captive

Keep me in the front of each thought and I will bring each thought captive so that destiny begins eternity.

*"For the weapons of our warfare are not carnal, but mighty through God to the pulling down of strong holds; Casting down imaginations, and every high thing that exalteth itself against the knowledge of God, and bringing into captivity every thought to the obedience of Christ."* (2 Corinthians 10:4-5 KJV)

Snuggle into my safety and know that nothing happens without me allowing it. I am always with you; walk in my light and shine for all to see that it is I walking with you.

*"Blessed are the people who know the joyful sound! They walk, O LORD, in the light of your countenance."* (Psalm 89:15)

Swim in my ocean of love and breathe me in like air in an airless world; I will be the bubbles around you. Grow up to meet the challenge I present to you and dare to climb with perseverance to finish well.

*"Truly the signs of an apostle were accomplished among you with all perseverance, in signs and wonders and mighty deeds."* (2 Corinthians 12:12)

# March 25th

**Faith**

Faith is the substance of things hoped for, the evidence of things about to be seen.

> *"Now faith is the substance of things hoped for, the evidence of things not seen."* (Hebrews 11:1)

Sitting with me brings wings to your vision and vision to your wings, directed by lavished, languished love. Peace is flowing down my back to pour into those who follow close behind me. Let me sweep you off your current patterns to carry you into a new season of colorful change.

**This Moment**

You can't see the end, and the beginning is not nearly as important as this moment you now give to me.

> *"He has made everything beautiful in its time. Also He has put eternity in their hearts, except that no one can find out the work that God does from beginning to end."* (Ecclesiastes 3:11)

I will reveal many secrets that will astonish your limited viewpoint, renewing and polishing your outlook. Where and when is not as important as what and how—this will be revealed in more dreams and visions.

## Revolution

Methods are good, but revolution is born from fresh new experiences. You will not need to rely on your own experience; just focus on experiencing me and new perspectives will emerge. Creation is never-ending in our thoughts, our hopes, and our dreams—so paint on my canvas and let me guide your brush. You are painting my face, and my face shines upon you for others to know I live. See more clearly my portrait, for it is a reflection of what I am creating in you.

# March 26th

## A Healing Explosion

*I attended a Healing Explosion event at the Church for all Nations in Tacoma, Washington where Bill Johnson from the Bethel Church in Redding, California was going to be speaking. The worship had already begun when I walked in the sanctuary, so I asked the Lord where I should sit. He told me to go to the front where people were standing and I quickly found a space in the front row. I glanced at the man standing next to me and became immediately aware that he carried a strong Christ-like presence. "I see Jesus in your eyes," I said. He thanked me and we hugged. Shortly afterwards, he walked up to the stage and I realized that he was the speaker—Bill Johnson. Although I had never met him or seen him before, I knew it was a divine encounter. What happened next was about to become a way of life....*

*Outside a blizzard was blowing and snow had blanketed the ground. In the same way, the Holy Spirit was blanketing the auditorium with his presence as we viewed a video of testimonies. Bill began to release the kingdom of Heaven in the room. I was skeptical because his methods were new to me; however, it wasn't long before I thought to myself that perhaps the Lord could release miracles through me. Many healings did happen that night, and I knew in my Spirit that this experience was for real. I was excited to put into practice what I had learned.*

## Washington Corrections Center for Women Story

*The next week, I was scheduled to speak at the Washington Corrections Center for Women in Purdy, Washington. The Lord had given me a strong, "Yes" when I asked him whether I should go, and then he gave me a vision of my friend, Stefan, handing me a piece of paper. I called him to ask him whether he'd like to go with me to the event, and he said he would. I asked, "Do you have something for me?" He responded, "Yes, I want to give you 'A Prayer of Release' [see Addendum]. I told him that I saw a vision of him giving me a piece of paper just as I was calling him.*

*I spoke in two services. The Lord instructed me to share two testimonies of people who had been healed when I prayed for them and said he would release healing into the room when I did. I was reminded of the verse in Revelation 12:11:*

> *"And they overcame him by the blood of the Lamb and the word of their testimony."*

*I spoke to the women: "I'm going to share two stories with you and the Spirit of God is going to pour into the room and many of you will be healed." The prison had issued a new ruling that stated visitors were not allowed to touch any of the women so healing could not be accomplished with the laying on of hands. I saw this as an opportunity to expand my faith. Twenty-three women were healed!*

## Reaction in the Prison

*After sharing these two testimonies, there was a reaction in the prison. Some women grabbed their necks, some their backs, and one woman* grabbed her foot. Headaches stopped, and only the Lord knows what else happened. All I know is that when I asked the women in the first service how many were physically healed in some part of their bodies, eleven hands went up, and some shared that they experienced heat and tingling. The scenario was repeated in the second service with twelve hands being raised. That's a total of twenty-three women who had been supernaturally touched by the Lord. Not one of those touched by the Spirit of God could be convinced that miracles don't happen today.

> "Jesus said to him, "Thomas, because you have seen me, you have believed. Blessed are those who have not seen and yet have believed."
> (John 20:29)

It's natural to live supernaturally. What's not natural is the absence of the supernatural.

## First Testimony

I was on a sidewalk and heard moaning, so I walked toward the sound and found a woman—Mary was her name, sitting on a chair. I said, "Are you okay?" She said, "No, I'm in terrible pain." "What happened?" I asked. She continued, "Several weeks ago, I fell down the marble stairs at work and I haven't been able to return because of the severe pain. The doctor put me on medication, but the pills aren't working! It hurts to sit, but it hurts worse to stand." I told her that the Lord loves her, and I believed he sent me to pray for her so she could be healed. "Can I pray for you?" She said, "Yes."

I placed my hand gently on her back and told her I would keep it there until the Lord told me the healing was done, and then I would take it off and she would be healed." "I command this back to be healed right now in the name of Jesus, every joint, every tendon—be perfectly aligned." She felt heat and a tingling up her spine. Moments later, when the Lord told me *it was done, I said, "It's done. Get up and try it out; it's totally healed." I removed my hands from her back.*

*She started dancing around her garage, crying and shouting and praising God—all pain was GONE! "Are you an angel?" she asked. I laughed and said, "No, I'm just a man who obeyed God's voice." Hearing the commotion, her teenage daughter rushed into the garage and gasped, "Mom, what are you doing?" Her mother said, "This man—this man—he healed me." I exclaimed, "No, the Lord brought the healing—I just did the praying!"*

## Second Testimony

*I was driving down the street in Eastern Washington when the Lord prompted me to stop at a certain house. I knocked on the door and a woman answered. Her name was Melissa. I gave her a brochure of a product I was selling. She thanked me and told me that her husband had been out of work for months because of an injury to his knee. I said, "We should pray for him because I believe God will heal him." She invited me in and introduced me to Michael. He was walking slowly to the kitchen, using his crutches. I shared with him that I had been praying for people and had seen many miracles. "I believe God is going to heal your knee. Can you sit down somewhere and we'll believe God will work a miracle? "Sure," he said. "Come on into the other room. We've been praying for four months." "That's okay; today is your day," I countered.*

*He sat in a chair and I asked his wife to come over and join him. Then I said, "This is what is going to happen: We're going to pray, believing in faith, and the Lord is going to heal this knee." I put both hands around his knee and began to thank God that he makes all things new and that nothing is impossible for those who believe. I commanded the knee to be fully restored in the mighty name of Jesus. I could feel the Holy Spirit pouring out power through my hands. Michael could feel heat pouring into his knee. He said, "It's getting hot!" "That's because it's getting healed," I responded. He started laughing with me. I said, "Now, stand up and take that thing for a walk!" He stood up and cautiously did some squats WITHOUT pain! In amazement, looking at his wife, he said, "It doesn't hurt—I mean really, it doesn't hurt—the pain is gone."*

*I said, "Let's go outside and you can walk around." I followed him down the hall and down the stairs and onto the lawn. Michael threw his hands up in the air, and with tears in his eyes, started running around the lawn, declaring, "I'm healed! I'm healed!" We were all filled with joy. Now he shared that it had been four months since his injury, he couldn't afford the suggested surgery, and as a result, he was unable to work his land, which was his livelihood. His marriage had been struggling because of his own discouragement and hopelessness. "But NOT anymore—now I can go back to work—now I can plow my field!"*

# March 27th

## Response to Life

Sometimes rain falls and life happens, but your response to it is the most important. Don't expect a life with no trouble; just know that I am with you in each situation, great or small. Plan on good times, and if bad times come, praise me and their visit will be shortened. Blessings flow to you, son—just receive them with open arms, one by one. I will reward every minute spent with me. Hear me or not, you will absorb my presence. It is my presence upon you that people will want, and I give you words from my Holy Spirit that amaze those who hear.

## Sow What?

Pleasant, pleasing, plunderous planter—sow what I put in your hand.

> "Do not be deceived, God is not mocked; for whatever a man sows, that he will also reap." (Galatians 6:7)

I have given you the power of life and death. Call the harvest forth and it will be so; call the result forth and it will come to pass.

> "Death and life are in the power of the tongue, and those who love it will eat its fruit." (Proverbs 18:21)

Then leap into the fullness of joy and dance in my presence; laugh and sing for walking close to the most high is worthy to be celebrated!

> *"Let them praise His name with the dance; Let them sing praises to Him with the timbrel and harp."* (Psalm 149:3)

## Consider the Elephant

Consider the elephant so large in stature, walking with such force and difficult to stop, but I tell you, you are more difficult to stop than one of these, for my Spirit is upon you and an army of elephants cannot stop you from doing what I ask. So move in boldness as the force of my Spirit makes a way for you wherever you go, according to my will and good purpose. Hang on tightly to me and loosely to the things of this world, and we will ride through the dangers of Africa and foreign lands with no fears of lions or of man.

## No Reason

My bubble of protection is upon you, and you will not die until the moment I have chosen. You are a mighty warrior in my massive army and we will not fail. Grab hold of all I tell you, for within each word is a purpose. I don't speak to you for no reason, and there's no reason one should doubt my voice. My sheep do hear my voice, and I will speak to each one.

> *"My sheep hear my voice, and I know them, and they follow me."* (John 10:27)

Not all people want to hear what I say because they fear giving up their sin; others don't hunger enough to seek with diligence. Blessed are those who will and do for they will receive heaven. Paradise waits with eager expectation for all to come into the secret place you have found.

> *"He who dwells in the secret place of the Most High shall abide under the shadow of the Almighty."* (Psalm 91:1)

Some look to religious leaders, who live among the tombs, for direction, and all they find is dead men's bones, but it is I who breathes life into the dead so the dead will live. Now rise up, you who were dead and go about your Father's purpose.

> *"And do not present your members as instruments of unrighteousness to sin, but present yourselves to God as being alive from the dead, and your members as instruments of righteousness to God."* (Romans 6:13)

## My Light Cannot Be Hidden

Keep my words on your lips. Do not worry about opposition; when it rises up, laugh inside, knowing it is shaping your character.

> *"He will yet fill your mouth with laughing, and your lips with rejoicing."* (Job 8:21)

Strength is a wonder increased in the eyes of holiness. Look and see yet another measure being poured out like heavy showers on dry, crusty land. Soak it in and absorb the expanse. Increase your ability to consume me, for my light cannot be hidden, nor can my mercy. Abounding in passion, my love is much bigger than the word that limits it. I will pour it out, even when the word has lost its meaning.

## Desperate for Me

If you're going to get desperate, why not be desperate for me, for it is I who responds to you with provision. Suffering people ask, "How long will this last?" but the right path has already been presented. The homeless ask, "How low can I go?" I say, turn from your pride and then you will be exalted. Some hold out their hands with bitter expectation; I hold out my arms with tender mercies.

> *"Let your tender mercies come to me, that I may live; for your law is my delight."* (Psalm 119:77)

A fool continues in the same fruitless patterns, but the wise look for answers apart from judgment.

> *"Understand, you senseless among the people; and you fools, when will you be wise?"* (Psalm 94:8)

On a cold night, many need blankets, but my peace brings the thickest comfort.

> *"The LORD will give strength to His people; the LORD will bless his people with peace."* (Psalm 29:11)

If there is a need, I am the answer, but the answer is not heard by the way of the wicked.

> *"The way of the wicked is like darkness; they do not know what makes them stumble."* (Proverbs 4:19)

## Heaven

Heaven is more than a state of mind, but every mind should be focused on heaven.

## I Am the Planter

I release many precious gifts, all of which bring forth seed.

*"He who continually goes forth weeping, bearing seed for sowing, shall doubtless come again with rejoicing, bringing his sheaves with him."* (Psalm 126:6)

I am the planter, and those who know me pay close attention to learn my ways. Investigate my claims and find concrete evidence, supported by the laws of the universe that I've set up. I draw you to my center like gravity, collecting what is air-born.

*March 28th*

**Remember These Things**

As you can see, I am full of grace; my mercy endures forever.

*"And the Word became flesh and dwelt among us, and we beheld His glory, the glory as of the only begotten of the Father, full of grace and truth."* (John 1:14)

If you experience any condemnation, it is not from me, for I do not condemn.

> *"There is therefore now no condemnation to those who are in Christ Jesus, who do not walk according to the flesh, but according to the Spirit."* (Romans 8:1)

You shall mount up on wings as the eagle, run and not grow weary.

> *"But those who wait on the LORD shall renew their strength; they shall mount up with wings like eagles, they shall run and not be weary, they shall walk and not faint."* (Isaiah 40:31)

When I pour out my life unto the land of plenty, abounding joy will flow from heaven and the gifts of my Spirit will be released for my people.

*"Even so you, since you are zealous for spiritual gifts, let it be for the edification of the church that you seek to excel."* (1 Corinthians 14:12)

You will not need to climb to reach the heavens; the heavens will be brought to you. Your worship will be increased, both in time and ability.

*"But the hour is coming, and now is, when the true worshipers will worship the Father in spirit and truth; for the Father is seeking such to worship Him."* (John 4:23)

Your understanding will be blessed and wisdom will be granted you. Remember, I can take this wisdom from you in the same way it is given, so carefully pursue a walk that is blameless, and know my grace abounds in mercy.

*"Therefore, beloved, looking forward to these things, be diligent to be found by Him in peace, without spot and blameless."* (2 Peter 3:14)

# March 30th

**Tree of Life**

I see a tree made of solid gold:

It does not labor or worry; nor does it grow impatient.

It cannot be moved by looters.

It cannot be cut from its roots.

Its minerals are made of joy and love.

It is sparkling with grace and mercy.

It shines with the bounty of heaven planted for the purpose of life. Even the winds are confused by its unwillingness to bend because it is as solid as the rock on which it stands.

The ground cannot shake it.

The world cannot explain it—it is the tree of life!

People cannot deny it.

Minds cannot conceive it.

Philosophers cannot comprehend it.

I am that I am that I am that all will see. The wonders of heaven project my light. I flow as the never-ending fountain that brings the recourse of life, and I will not be removed.

I am rising up my fortress.

I am bringing my judgment, and I will see you through love and grace.

I will see you in heaven.

April 2011

*April 1st*

## People who Hurt

Go easy on my people when they fall short in understanding. Everyone is in a different stage of development, and many see life through a wounded past; their view of themselves and others is skewed by a hurting soul. The mind is the faculty that makes decisions, and the ability to make decisions is affected by a hurting soul. People who hurt are also afraid of failure; they don't like to be told they are wrong so they have a hard time receiving any criticism, constructive or not.

## False Protection

Pride often forms a false protection; it builds a wall or barrier to protect from future pain. Many times you will see isolation and a tendency to push others away, and depression is usually the result. Forgiveness, love, grace and mercy, along with acceptance, are great tools for building a ladder that can bridge the gap between rejection and abuse. Forgiveness of self and forgiveness of others is essential and must take place for healing to work. We must be able to identify what emotions need healing in order to make progress.

**Ask**

If you ask me, I will answer you and you will know how to pray—then I will hear your request and answer you according to my will.

*"And whatever things you ask in prayer, believing, you will receive."* (Matthew 21:22)

The secret to knowing how to pray is learning my will:

My will is to heal;

My will is to make all things new;

My will is to restore; my will is to bring together;

My will is clear.

I build. Who destroys?

I create. Who copies?

I plan prosperity. Who plans poverty?

I resurrect. Who brings death?

# April 4th

## As the Sun Is Rising

Don't give up your time with me; it will be the most important thing you do all day so put it first so it is not made last. Does it make sense to start out on a journey and then ask for direction toward its end? Then let us join together as the sun is rising so I can direct your day. I will give you instruction.

## You Will Reap What You Did Not Sow

I tell you the truth: The seed has been in the ground ready to bring forth life. You will reap what you did not sow in goodness and plenty. You are in the land to which I brought you, and you are about to realize my fullness. Expect what I tell you, for my plan is divine, my purpose is being fulfilled, and your destiny is at hand. I fill you now with an increased measure to reward this time you give to me. Thank you, my servant. Thank you for the sacrifice you bring—it pleases me. Do you know that you please me? I would not have it any other way. Now spend time with your daughter and delight in her as I delight in you.

# April 5th

## Lend a Hand

Pay attention to what goes on around you and look for opportunities to lend a hand as unto me.

> *"Whatever your hand finds to do, do it with your might; for there is no work or device or knowledge or wisdom in the grave where you are going."* (Ecclesiastes 9:10)

Don't allow yourself to get rocked by people who are rocked; just remain silent and pray for them. Be certain that you don't speak out of unholy anger toward people who offend you; just bless them and keep your peace. Take heed and hear me when I say: We have much to do.

## The Book: It's NOT Meant to Be a Secret

Great men with power and influence will be rocked by what this collection brings:

Faith will be increased;

Religious boxes will be blown apart;

Limited religious insight will be exposed, and

Many will receive the gift of real life in me.

Life-breathing joy will be released in each page; readers from all walks and religions will glean from its pages; it will shake the ground of strongholds, and bring forth my heart of love. The dry crust will crack open and living water will pour from its pages.

## Tend to My Garden

Cling to my words; keep them in your heart; resist temptation and rise up—I say it again: Rise up from the old ways; they no longer define you, for my definition is being revealed. If you are not sure, read it again until you understand; then walk deeper with me. Exchange the old and I will trade it with the new. Mountains tremble at my present happenings; the earth reports my moving hand. Record the seismic activity of my Spirit, shaking loose the frailty of sin. When a monument rises, erecting perpetual remembrance, destroy it for it has no place in my garden of forgiveness and grace. See to it that you tend to my garden; it is shaped like a heart; plant:

Goodness,

Love,

Kindness,

Gentleness,

Meekness, and

Humility.

Post warrior angels to guard it from looters and thieves. See to it that no stranger comes to toss bad seed into it.

## You Are My Masterpiece

Be still and think on what I've told you because you are my masterpiece, and I do not want anyone's hand to touch my work before I complete it. You are being made solid. Don't worry about what has not happened; I have said that it's part of my process. Go now and share with your beautiful wife.

## Why Don't You See?

Do you not know that I am the God of miracles? Or have you not witnessed my goodness? Stop your practical thinking. My ways have nothing to do with present circumstances. Why don't you listen to me? Why don't you see the things of the Spirit? I tell you, your childhood has tainted your view of me; disappointment has settled into your soul so you think you cannot experience your dream. I tell you: You will not realize what you dream if you expect to fail. Put your hope in someone greater than your past—someone greater than you—and be bold to step out on faith, believing in what is to come.

> *"Why are you cast down, O my soul? And why are you disquieted within me? Hope in God, for I shall yet praise him for the help of his countenance."* (Psalm 42:5)

You will not enter into my promise by whining and complaining, but by praising and thanking me for what you see in the Spirit.

> *"Now therefore, our God, we thank you and praise your glorious name."* (1 Chronicles 29:13)

Saddle up your horses and let's ride on. There is a balance of good planning and believing that has to occur.

*"There is no one like the God of Jeshurun, who rides the heavens to help you, And in his Excellency on the clouds."* (Deuteronomy 33:26)

## Jesus Speaks to Cosette, My Eight-Year-Old Daughter

You are making progress at becoming a great artist, and you will also become an amazing singer. You, like your father, will write songs that will be celebrated around the world. It is a new season for you to enjoy the importance of honesty. I am teaching you so many important lessons. You have many special talents, and I have made you beautiful as well, and I delight in the way you play about.

You are learning a lot about me, and one thing you should know is that many reject who I am, but I will use you to tell them about me. Never be ashamed of me.

*"For I am not ashamed of the gospel of Christ, for it is the power of God to salvation for everyone who believes, for the Jew first and also for the Greek."* (Romans 1:16)

Because you know me, I will give you a new perspective or another way to look at things. Don't worry so much about being approved and accepted because I was cast down and rejected and still suffer persecution.

*"He is despised and rejected by men, a man of sorrows and acquainted with grief. And we hid, as it were, our faces from Him; he was despised, and we did not esteem him."* (Isaiah 53:3)

It's okay if people don't like you because you know me. I love you so much, and I took away all your sins when I died on the cross, and because I rose again, I gave you the power to overcome your problems.

*"But as many as received him, to them gave he power to become the sons of God, even to them that believe on his name."* (John 1:12)

I hold you close to me as my own precious daughter, and I love your smile. You have my joy and holy laughter, and I will pour myself out for you to enjoy. Sit with me and we will read together, color together, and play together. I am with you always and will never leave you.

*"For He Himself has said, "I will never leave you nor forsake you."*
(Hebrews 13:5)

Stay close to me and absorb my love because it is endless. I will help you in school so don't worry; just trust in me and life will go smoother. Problems are opportunities for growth and improvement, so just let them happen, and look to me for your answers and solutions. Be loving to people, but don't worry about having all the attention all the time; just know that I am your friend and I want you to make me your best friend.

*"No longer do I call you servants, for a servant does not know what his master is doing; but I have called you friends, for all things that I heard from my Father I have made known to you."* (John 15:15)

# April 6th

## Harvest Power

Power is harvested in spending time with me. Be sure not to judge others to condemn them; only judge to evaluate, but be gentle in your evaluation, extending grace, and I will be more gracious onto you.

*"Judge not, and you shall not be judged. Condemn not, and you shall not be condemned. Forgive, and you will be forgiven."* (Luke 6:37)

Keep my promises wrapped around your heart as a protection from all bitterness.

*"Pursue peace with all people, and holiness, without which no one will see the Lord: looking carefully lest anyone fall short of the grace of God; lest any root of bitterness springing up cause trouble, and by this many become defiled."* (Hebrews 12:14-15)

## Send Angels

Sending my angels out is an important tool to get things done in the Spirit. Many don't take advantage of this truth. I know you have seen results, but I want you to do it more often, for I have assigned many angels—equipped and ready—for battle and duty. Send them and they will obey your command; they do not tire of serving you.

> *"Bless the LORD, you his angels, who excel in strength, who do his word, heeding the voice of His word."* (Psalm 103:20)

> *"The Son of Man will send out his angels, and they will gather out of his kingdom all things that offend, and those who practice lawlessness."* (Matthew 13:41)

> *"And I will give you the keys of the kingdom of heaven, and whatever you bind on earth will be bound in heaven, and whatever you loose on earth will be loosed in heaven."* (Matthew 16:19)

This will be very important in the days ahead. **You must battle things of the Spirit with things of the Spirit** and you will benefit in the physical. It is not some dream land—it is the reality of what I have established.

> *"For we do not wrestle against flesh and blood, but against principalities, against powers, against the rulers of the darkness of this age, against spiritual hosts of wickedness in the heavenly places."* (Ephesians 6:12)

## April 7th

### Roots and Soil

Roots and soil—soil and roots; does what you plant really make a difference? Good seed will always produce good fruit; bad seed will always produce bad fruit.

> *Therefore hear the parable of the sower: When anyone hears the word of the kingdom, and does not understand it, then the wicked one comes and snatches away what was sown in his heart. This is he who received seed by the wayside. But he who received the seed on stony places, this is he who hears the word and immediately receives it with joy; yet he has no root in himself, but endures only for a while. For when tribulation or persecution arises because of the word, immediately he stumbles. Now he who received seed among the thorns is he who hears the word, and the cares of this world and the deceitfulness of riches choke the word, and he becomes unfruitful. But he who received seed on the good ground is he who hears the word and understands it, who indeed bears fruit and produces: some a hundredfold, some sixty, some thirty.*" (Matthew 13:18-23)

If you wonder whether you should enter an agreement with someone, check his fruit—is it good?

*"If a man makes a vow to the LORD, or swears an oath to bind himself by some agreement, he shall not break his word; he shall do according to all that proceeds out of his mouth."* (Numbers 30:2)

If you hear me, then it's much better to ask me. You know my voice. "Know them by their fruit" is a message to those who are still learning to hear me. Since you are hearing my voice so clearly, just ask me.

*"Beware of false prophets, who come to you in sheep's clothing, but inwardly they are ravenous wolves. You will know them by their fruits. Do men gather grapes from thorn bushes or figs from thistles?"* (Matthew 7:15-16)

Always bind the Stranger's voice[1] before we talk and listen to what I say closely so you don't miss anything.

*"And when he brings out his own sheep, he goes before them; and the sheep follow him, for they know his voice. Yet they will by no means follow a stranger, but will flee from him, for they do not know the voice of strangers."* (John 10:4-5)

---

1  "Stranger" is a term for Satan or one of his demons.

# April 8th

**Uncover My Secrets**

You marvel at my innermost secrets as I marvel at your faith.

 It is strong, filled up, and childlike.

My secrets are meant to be uncovered;

 My mysteries are meant to be revealed.

You ask me in secret, and I answer you in the open

 Because my ways are to be shared.

My love is to be released to the full;

 Pour me out like gushing streams.

Let my raging rivers rise within you;

 Quaking banks of progress share their timeless wisdom.


My roots will never wither; my peace will never die.

 Giving all my goodness, I cannot tell a lie.

Life flows from my ankles and pours into the ground.

   The essence of my presence is blessing all who've found.

Standing in the doorway of open hearts I see

   Many grown from silence; the prince who's clearly free;

Picking up the pieces of every passing storm;

   Placing them with newness; leaving many to be warned.

Ride the wake I leave you; it carries you abroad

   To the next town that I bring you; some find it very odd

How you can hear so clearly what I have now to say.

   You came to me so hungry and I've answered what you prayed.

## God Gives Me a Message for One of His Children...

My precious daughter: you have endured enough pain. I have prepared you to speak from your experience with pain. I want to heal your body, but I need your cooperation. I will not take your friends away from you—you must willingly give them over to me. Pain killers are a counterfeit pain relief. Give them over to me and allow me to heal you. I will be your new prescription. I need your mind to be sharp in order to carry out my purpose. I will not set you free from what you have made a friend.

   *"Therefore if the Son makes you free, you shall be free indeed."*
   (John 8:36)

I love you. I do not condemn you.

*"There is therefore now no condemnation to those who are in Christ Jesus, who do not walk according to the flesh, but according to the Spirit."* (Romans 8:1)

I sit with you and see all your frustration.

Spend time with me.

Talk with me.

Ask of me.

I desire to restore your body. I will bring you into a new season, for behold, I am coming soon. Let nothing hinder your progress, for I will release upon you my fullness. Your family will see what I have done in you and will rejoice and sing with shouts of joy. Your enemy will not prevail against you for I, the Lord your God, am with you.

Thank you for your faithful service

To me,

To my children, and

To my people.

Now, prepare yourself for freedom; make time for me. Turn off the TV and give me your time, for there is much to do. I will speak and you will hear. I am healing your brain and clarity will be the result.

## Bring Forth My Rhythms

Peace is restoring the broken,

Torment melting like springtime snow,

Jagged mountains of love and mercy erupt from seas of grace.

All my designs are passing the open expanse;

Whether bouncing in and out—the changes never ceasing.

But one thing—yes one thing—remains the same:

I, the Lord your God, creator of heaven and earth,

Spreading my music on you like a symphony,

Strings learning their placement,

Notes finding a home,

I pour out my orchestration.


Play deep within the Spirit;

Bring forth my rhythms;

Dive deep into the beat of heaven;

Hold on to heaven's gate.


I increase your talents—

Cast them toward the hungry ears of those desperate for life.

Share the melodies of my heart's song.

Continually dig deep into me.

I release upon you now the melodies.

You don't have any dryness or shortage because I give you many new
songs:

Songs as smooth as water,

   Songs of healing and life

      Bring forth my bounty;

         Pour out my phrases.


Keep gathering the pieces.

   Holy heavens join your praise,

      Anointed to overflowing with godly living streams

         Pounding down their goodness;

            Bursting at their seams.


It is not possible to contain the fullness that I bring;

   Gushing hearts of passion releasing all to sing.

      Don't try to keep it—just give it all away;

         I have long prepared you for this very day.


One more thing:

   You could not even begin to imagine the depth of my love for you.

      You're not designed to comprehend fully

         But I am expanding your ability to conceive.

*April 9th*

**Nothing Done in Secret Will Avoid Exposure**

People will not like to have their sins revealed, but I tell you that nothing done in secret will be able to avoid exposure, but all will be laid bare by me and accounted for.

*"For there is nothing hidden which will not be revealed, nor has anything been kept secret but that it should come to light."* (Mark 4:22)

Victory is conceived first in the mind of understanding and then dances to the surface of those who've been trained by it. A full measure is a unit being properly bestowed upon the one who will receive.

*"For whatever is born of God overcomes the world. And this is the victory that has overcome the world—our faith."* (1 John 5:4)

**Unbelief Prevents Hearing**

Many would love to hear me, but they are not convinced that I will speak. Not believing that I'll speak is unbelief, and it prevents ears from hearing. Take off your unbelief, you deaf nation, and I will speak again, and what I tell you will break through the fog of your unfaithfulness.

*"For what if some did not believe? Will their unbelief make the faithfulness of God without effect?"* (Romans 3:3)

Stay in me and I will guide your steps. Go on your own, pursuing your deceitful lusts, and destruction will be your end. When will you give up your torment?

*"But you have not so learned Christ, if indeed you have heard Him and have been taught by Him, as the truth is in Jesus: that you put off, concerning your former conduct, the old man which grows corrupt according to the deceitful lusts, and be renewed in the spirit of your mind, and that you put on the new man which was created according to God, in true righteousness and holiness."* (Ephesians 4:20-24)

## Definition of My Church

My church is any group that gets together on a regular basis for the study of my word and participates in praise and worship.

## Words to a Pastor

If a branch falls from my tree, it will surely die unless it is a seed—then it will surely carry on my life source. Don't worry about competition; just keep planting seeds. Sow into my kingdom where the fruit of duplication lives. The fruit that falls from my tree represents overflowing. Broken fruit exposes seed—seed that produces an extensive harvest. Your work is an extension of me, and I see life spreading to the ends of the earth. Just hand out the fruit; don't try to count the apples. Some will carry those seeds to the ends of the earth; the delivery is my business—don't worry if they don't return. There are different systems of measurement in my kingdom. I want you to remember that I, the

Lord your God, love you with a greater capacity than you were made to understand.

What I am preparing to unleash inside of you is more than what you have imagined. Keep your faith—your ministry effort has reached much farther than your ears can hear. You are mighty in my kingdom, son of Jacob. Be encouraged this day and know that I will tap on every religious box until my order is all that stands. There will be many boxes to burst open—none flowing with water—each labeled separately:

Theology,

Psychology,

Religiosity, and

Pride.

The final box we will break open together! Drawing down the rod, it will burst open. You will hit solid rock and you will know this is the place to stand. You can see I have much to say and you will hear me.

My peace is filling you now:

My joy poured out in increasing measure,

My love is rising in you like the ocean—

Ride my wave or be swallowed up by it.

You are my child in whom I am well pleased.

Keep pressing in.

Keep pressing on.

Quiet time is no waste of time.

I see you,

I sit with you,

I delight in you, smiling.

Knowledge is important—it can be learned, but wisdom is a gift from heaven. Ask and I shall increase your measure.

*"If any of you lacks wisdom, let him ask of God, who gives to all liberally and without reproach, and it will be given to him."* (James 1:5)

Suicide is a spirit and deliverance is not popular but necessary. You are dealing with a network of demonic forces:

Suicide,

Discouragement,

Despair,

Hopelessness,

Depression, and

Murder.

Keep my love in balance because my love casts out the Spirit of Fear and victory is always the result.

*"There is no fear in love; but perfect love casts out fear, because fear involves torment. But he who fears has not been made perfect in love."* (1 John 4:18)

*"For God has not given us a spirit of fear, but of power and of love and of a sound mind."* (2 Timothy 1:7)

Put your stake in the ground; declare what I have asked of you; decree what will happen. Testimony builds faith—faith is what I require. Review and release the testimonies of the lambs—the victory is mine to be shared!

*"And this is the testimony: that God has given us eternal life, and this life is in His Son."* (1 John 5:11)

## A Word Given to Me for a Young Man

I know the pressures you are under. I see you ponder as you look at the sky. I know there are many difficult decisions you need to make. Your battle is not against what you see, but what you don't see.

*"For we do not wrestle against flesh and blood, but against principalities, against powers, against the rulers of the darkness of this age, against spiritual hosts of wickedness in the heavenly places."* (Ephesians 6:12)

I will teach you to fight with the power of my Holy Spirit, and you will win because I am with you. You ask me to heal you, and my answer is: Turn from all wicked behavior and resist the Devil and he will flee from you.

*"Therefore submit to God. Resist the devil and he will flee from you."* (James 4:7)

You experience torment and I will deliver you.

*"Then His fame went throughout all Syria; and they brought to Him all sick people who were afflicted with various diseases and torments, and those who were demon-possessed, epileptics, and paralytics; and He healed them."* (Matthew 4:24)

I have chosen your future wife and will reveal her when you are ready. I heard your surrender—now invite me to come in and lead you and you will become a part of the ultimate adventure. I desire to bless you with good health, joy, and peace. Let me guide your life; learn to trust me more. I will train you in my ways. Don't be afraid—we will do this together.

I will heal your mind, your will, and your emotions. You will experience my perfect peace. I hear your cries and I answer with comfort. I am the Lord your God, maker of heaven and earth. Do not be deceived in your mind; allow me to transform you.

*"And do not be conformed to this world, but be transformed by the renewing of your mind, that you may prove what is that good and acceptable and perfect will of God."* (Romans 12:2)

I will take your anger and turn it into gladness.

*"Let all bitterness, wrath, anger, clamor, and evil speaking be put away from you, with all malice."* (Ephesians 4:31)

Be on guard not to be seduced by worldly philosophy.

*"Beware lest anyone cheat you through philosophy and empty deceit, according to the tradition of men, according to the basic principles of the world, and not according to Christ."* (Colossians 2:8)

Read Matthew, Mark, Luke, and John.

See me,

Know me,

Love me as I have first loved you.

Your earthly father can let you down, but I will never leave you nor forsake you. I am with you now; keep my promises close to your heart; nothing is impossible for me.

It is my desire that you mount up on wings like the eagle and that you run and not grow weary.

> *"But those who wait on the LORD shall renew their strength; they shall mount up with wings like eagles, they shall run and not be weary, they shall walk and not faint."* (Isaiah 40:31)

I love you just the way you are. I accept you if you changed nothing, but I am a rewarder of those who obey.

> *"But without faith it is impossible to please Him, for he who comes to God must believe that He is, and that He is a rewarder of those who diligently seek Him."* (Hebrews 11:6)

My will will be done on earth as it is in heaven.

> *"So He said to them, "When you pray, say: Our Father in heaven, Hallowed be your name. Your kingdom come. Your will be done on earth as it is in heaven."* (Luke 11:2)

There are many traps set for you—I will help you expose them, one by one.

> *"Keep me from the snares they have laid for me, And from the traps of the workers of iniquity."* (Psalm 141:9)

You are going to find your purpose in me; you are going to know me deeper than you ever imagined. Fear not the unknown—just learn of me for I am meek and lowly in heart and there you will find rest for your soul.

*"Take my yoke upon you and learn from me, for I am gentle and lowly in heart, and you will find rest for your souls."*
(Matthew 11:29)

## Words to a Family

This family is important to me—my desire is to speak to each one. I want all of you to know me more; I want to heal your broken parts, to pour out my love upon you that you would see my goodness. Do not be blind to the schemes of the Destroyer. Learn about me so you understand my ways, but more importantly, know me like I know you. Many of you have experienced my fullness, but some have rejected me because of the influences around you that have rejected me. People who reject me do so out of selfish ignorance. If you knew me, you would know I have a plan, a purpose for each one of you.

*"And we know that all things work together for good to those who love God, to those who are called according to His purpose."*
(Romans 8:28)

Surrender to me and lack no good thing.

Let me fill you;

Let me love you;

Let me heal your bodies of pain, deep within your souls.

Security is found in the one who makes you secure, Jesus, the risen savior. Oh, how I long to rescue this fallen nation, but they won't lift their hands to me. I need cooperation.

*I see a vision of a helicopter rescue plane swooping down to rescue a man.*

Do you really know better than me, the creator of all heaven and earth? Do not be deceived any more—I have come to give you life and more abundantly.

I can see the bad seed that's been sown into the lives of our young people. Now I say,

"Young people—wake up from your passive state;

Wake up and hear me.

Tend to the garden that is your mind—

It is connected to the soul.

Turn your will toward me and experience freedom;

Let me heal your emotions.

Pull every seed from its root so your garden will flourish.

Let go of bitterness;

Let go of pride;

Let go of selfishness;

Let go of your anger!"

I am bringing this family into a new season—

One of rejoicing;

One of celebration.

Do not avoid gathering together and be willing to learn from one another. We can learn from the young and the old alike. Let me show you my design—it is far better than you thought. Be willing to surrender everything that hinders and run the race that is set before you.

> *"Therefore we also, since we are surrounded by so great a cloud of witnesses, let us lay aside every weight, and the sin which so easily ensnares us, and let us run with endurance the race that is set before us."* (1 Corinthians 9:24)

I want you to win. I want you to share in the rewards and riches of heaven. It is not fantasy—it is as real as I who speak to you now. Some of you are experiencing unbelief, but I tell you, a little faith will go a long way, so use what measure you have and I will increase it.

> *"So the Lord said, "If you have faith as a mustard seed, you can say to this mulberry tree, 'Be pulled up by the roots and be planted in the sea,' and it would obey you."* (Luke 17:6)

I love you so very much. Stay with me; don't shift in and out like the tide. Stay all in and you will experience life to the full.

## The Lord Asks Me to Give this Message to a Teenage Girl

I sent you a letter in my Bible and it remains on your desk unopened. It's time to know the truth about me. You have been influenced by this world that has rejected me, but I am revealing unto you my fullness of life. I have chosen your spouse. He is in love with me and is very handsome. Don't settle for Mr. Wrong when I have prepared Mr. Right.

Protect yourself from harm by coming to me. I tell you the truth; no darkness can stand in the presence of my light. Come to me, child; I will protect you from harm. I see your beautiful future and I call on your steps. Trust me even if your role model does not, and I will give you wisdom beyond your years. Your beauty is not meant for yourself;

it is meant to lead people to me, the Lord your God, maker of heaven and earth.

Don't miss what I have for you, my child. I love you so much—allow me to show you. I accept the way you are, apart from your own performance. I have made you worthy at the cross. I have given you the power of life and death, and it is released with your tongue. I will heal your hurting soul. I will give you the keys to my kingdom. You are special and unique. I have fashioned you in your mother's womb.

*"Before I formed you in the womb I knew you…"* (Jeremiah 1:5)

I am opening doors before you; come to me and I will release on you every good thing. I see you and I delight in watching you learn and grow. Be not discouraged; be not angry; just walk in forgiveness of yourself and others and I will heal your broken heart. Let me love you.

*"The LORD is near to those who have a broken heart, and saves such as have a contrite spirit."* (Psalm 34:18)

*April 14th*

## A Message Given to Me for a Husband

Seek me and you will find me if you seek me with your whole heart—I need your whole heart.

*"With my whole heart I have sought you; Oh, let me not wander from Your commandments!"* (Psalm 119:10)

You have surrendered most of it, but I want all of it; then you will surely experience life to the full. Don't worry about money and the systems of this world; they cannot prevent my blessing.

*"For the love of money is a root of all kinds of evil, for which some have strayed from the faith in their greediness, and pierced themselves through with many sorrows."* (1 Timothy 6:10)

Stay faithful with that which is least and I will trust you with much more.

*"And he said to him, 'Well done, good servant; because you were faithful in a very little, have authority over ten cities."* (Luke 19:17)

Do not give in to the Spirit of Fear, for it moves hell, but faith is what moves heaven on earth.

*"For God has not given us a spirit of fear, but of power and of love and of a sound mind."* (2 Timothy 1:7)

Call what is not seen, as though it is, and your circumstance will change for the better.

*"But hope that is seen is not hope; for why does one still hope for what he sees? But if we hope for what we do not see, we eagerly wait for it with perseverance."* (Romans 8:24-25)

I have given you a measure of faith, and I increase your measure now.

Thank you for adjusting your lifestyle. I am removing that which is shakable in you so I can build on that which is solid.

*"He is like a man building a house, who dug deep and laid the foundation on the rock. And when the flood arose, the stream beat vehemently against that house, and could not shake it, for it was founded on the rock."* (Luke 6:48)

I want to build your marriage stronger. I want you to learn how to value your wife. She is so precious to me; if only you could see her the way I see her.

*"He who finds a wife finds a good thing, and obtains favor from the* LORD.*"* (Proverbs 18:22)

You are my magnificent caretaker; I saw you tending to the needs of your siblings, shepherding them, offering yourself to them with protection. I tell you the truth: you are precious in my sight. Keep doing as unto me and know that I am with you.

My love is surrounding you now; my direction is at hand. I am preparing you for a unique adventure in ministry. You will go when I send you and join my effort to seek and to save the lost. Many will come to know me because you are willing to go.

*"For the Son of Man has come to seek and to save that which was lost."* (Luke 19:10)

Spend more time with me alone; do not be discouraged. I see you sitting, praying for a while, and then going on getting busy. Stay with me without distraction. Let me share the keys to my kingdom so you can unlock my fullness.

*"And I will give you the keys of the kingdom of heaven, and whatever you bind on earth will be bound in heaven, and whatever you loose on earth will be loosed in heaven."* (Matthew 16:19)

My house has many rooms—we will explore them together. This is going to be so much fun!

*"In my Father's house are many mansions; if it were not so, I would have told you. I go to prepare a place for you."* (John 14:2)

I want your time, your thoughts and your whole heart.

*"Blessed are those who keep His testimonies, who seek Him with the whole heart!"* (Psalm 119:2)

Let the great adventure begin today, the first day of the rest of your life. Peace flows from heaven to fill you with my Holy presence. I love you so much. You were not designed to comprehend it.

*"This is my commandment, that you love one another as I have loved you."* (John 15:12)

Let me teach you,

Guide you,

Direct you—I will give you instructions.

## A Message Given to Me for a Wife

You do so much with a gracious attitude. I did not intend for you to feel like a slave, but to be free. Your situation is most temporary, for I am preparing you for full-time service to me. Your work ethic is excellent, but when you do work for me, you will not feel as though you are working. Finish well this tax season, and I will give you instructions, for I have been preparing you and your husband for greatness. You have been groomed for my service and you will be well taken care of. Don't allow your boss to get you frantic inside; just pace yourself and build in boundaries. Do what you can and put your foot down more often and my peace will come in the rest of my Spirit.

I love you more than you know how to understand. Soon the winds will settle and the storm will pass. Learn to operate from my rest. Transfer to me your burden and I will gladly accept its weight.

> *"Take my yoke upon you and learn from me, for I am gentle and lowly in heart, and you will find rest for your souls. For my yoke is easy and my burden is light."* (Matthew 11:29-30)

Your heart is so beautiful; your countenance is so sweet.

> *"A merry heart makes a cheerful countenance, But by sorrow of the heart the spirit is broken."* (Proverbs 15:13)

Spend more time with me alone, for I wish to speak to you and instruct you in your coming and in your going. This will be difficult at first, but pencil me in and it will be the thing you grow to value above all else.

> *"The LORD shall preserve your going out and your coming in from this time forth, and even forevermore."* (Psalm 121:8)

# April 15th

## The Lord Asks Me to Fast

*Lord, I'm sorry I didn't fast when you asked me to.*

When you fail to obey my request, just start again.

> *"Do not rejoice over me, my enemy; when I fall, I will arise; when I sit in darkness, the LORD will be a light to me."* (Micah 7:8)

I want you to start now; juice fast today and listen for my voice.

> *"But the days will come when the bridegroom will be taken away from them, and then they will fast in those days."* (Mark 2:20)

I will give you more instructions throughout the day.

## A Message Given to Me for Another

You are precious to me, my daughter. Even though you are often misunderstood, I understand you completely. Remember all I have brought you through, and know this is not the end but only the beginning. I am revealing myself to you in greater measure. It is my desire to heal your body. You have thought you must deserve this infirmity, but I say I am your deliverer, and I will heal the broken hearts of my children. I see you sitting, wondering about how you could have done things differently, but where you've been is not nearly as important as where you are headed. Stay in my peace and allow me to comfort you.

Your gifts are mighty, for I am the one who has gifted you—not so that you would keep them to yourself, or your close family, but that you would face your fears and share them with the world. Do you not know that my plans for you are greater than your plans for yourself? Seek me and you will find me when you seek me with all your heart.

*"And you will seek me and find me, when you search for me with all your heart."* (Jeremiah 29:13)

Know me and you will grow more and more in my love.

*"But let him who glories glory in this, that he understands and knows me, that I am the LORD, exercising loving-kindness, judgment, and righteousness in the earth. For in these I delight," says the LORD.* (Jeremiah 9:24)

You have been turned off by the religious practices of man and the hypocrisy that has hurt you, but remember that I am your friend, the one who has fashioned you in your mother's womb. I will never leave you nor forsake you, child. I love you. I accept you just the way you are. Come and learn of me, for I am meek and lowly in heart and you will find rest for your hurting soul.

*"Take my yoke upon you, and learn of me; for I am meek and lowly in heart: and ye shall find rest unto your souls."* (Matthew 11:29 KJV)

Forgive others as I have forgiven you, and let your life blossom this spring with newness of life. Think of me often, for not a moment goes by that I don't think of you. Know my son, Jesus, and you will know the truth and find life to the full, uncontainable and running over with abounding joy.

*"And you shall know the truth, and the truth shall make you free."*
(John 8:32)

I am the giver of peace; my presence is a present.

*"Now to Him who is able to keep you from stumbling, and to present you faultless before the presence of his glory with exceeding joy, to God our Savior, who alone is wise, be glory and majesty, dominion and power, both now and forever. Amen." (Jude 1:24-25)*

I give you a new song—a song of freedom, a song of restoration.

*"He has put a new song in my mouth—Praise to our God; Many will see it and fear, and will trust in the LORD." (Psalm 40:3)*

You have been friendly to those who have wronged you—well done, well done!

*"But I say to you, love your enemies, bless those who curse you, do good to those who hate you, and pray for those who spitefully use you and persecute you." (Matthew 5:44)*

I watch you arise with optimism and I smile. When the spirit of fear rises up, I laugh for it has no power over me; my love sends it running for cover, and so it will be with you, daughter. Cling to my truth; let it be active in you that all will know I live. Give me your worries and let me turn them into stories of triumph. I do not force my ways on you, but offer you love unspeakable and joy abounding.

*"Whom having not seen, ye love; in whom, though now ye see him not, yet believing, ye rejoice with joy unspeakable and full of glory."*
(1 Peter 1:8 KJV)

Read my love letter and absorb my countenance as it is I who is setting you free. Do not doubt me; just press in and press on, and breakthrough will be the result. Blessed are you, my child. You hear my voice and the volume will increase. The clarity will be as if you were hearing the ocean with its variance of sounds and tones.

I will speak to you through others;

    I will speak in your circumstances, and

      I will speak through my word to you.

I give you now ears to hear; I give you now eyes to see, better than before, better than ever before. My voice is water to your thirsty soul. Let it satisfy you always.

*"I spread out my hands to you; my soul longs for you like a thirsty land. Selah."* (Psalm 143:6)

Be being filled with my Holy presence until you lack no good thing.

*"And do not be drunk with wine, in which is dissipation; but be filled with the Spirit."* (Ephesians 5:18)

Yes, it is I who speaks to you now—it is I.

*April 16th*

## Forgiving Others

*The Lord gave me this word for a specific person, but we all have the need to know and understand the importance of forgiving others.*

Do you not know my love covers your sin? Do you not know that I have forgiven you? Why do you not forgive others?

> *"Take heed to yourselves. If your brother sins against you, rebuke him; and if he repents, forgive him."* (Luke 17:3)

Free yourself in this and see that freedom reigns in those released by it. Release yourself from condemnation, for who is it who condemns? Surely, it is not the one who died for your sins and rose again to bring you victory.

> *"There is therefore now no condemnation to those who are in Christ Jesus, who do not walk according to the flesh, but according to the Spirit."* (Romans 8:1)

Walk in forgiveness of others as I have forgiven you and you will be free of wrongful judgment.

> *"Judge not, that you be not judged."* (Matthew 7:1)

My peace is meant to be shared. Find its fullness; then share from love and acceptance just as I have accepted you and showered you with love and mercy.

I was there when you were hurt as a child. It was not my will, but I have given free will. I love you the way you are—receive my truth and release a fresh outlook. View yourself as:

Free,

Redeemed, and

Forgiven.

But do not think of yourself more highly than you ought, for then pride can come to cause you to fall.

> *"For I say, through the grace given to me, to everyone who is among you, not to think of himself more highly than he ought to think, but to think soberly, as God has dealt to each one a measure of faith."* (Romans 12:3)

Bow before me and surrender your own will and I will lift you up in a new beginning. Go to those you have hurt and ask forgiveness, and I will forgive your sins and bring forth good fruit.

> *"Take heed to yourselves. If your brother sins against you, rebuke him; and if he repents, forgive him."* (Luke 17:3)

Do not forgive and you yourself cannot be fully forgiven. Walk in forgiveness that no bitter root can be raised up against you.

> *"Pursue peace with all people, and holiness, without which no one will see the Lord: looking carefully lest anyone fall short of the grace*

*of God; lest any root of bitterness springing up cause trouble, and by this many become defiled."* (Hebrews 12:14-15)

Let me heal your wounded soul; it has altered your perception of yourself and others. Be of one mind and bind the demonic forces of schizophrenia for double-minded people are unstable in all their ways.

*"He is a double-minded man, unstable in all his ways."* (James 1:8)

I pour out on you new understanding. Let me lead you in planting good seed, for if you do not, destruction will be all that results. Blessed are those who hunger and thirst for righteousness, for theirs is the kingdom of Heaven.

*"Blessed are those who hunger and thirst for righteousness, for they shall be filled."* (Matthew 5:6)

You have received me, but now it is time to make me Lord, or do you know better than I do, maker of heaven and earth? Surrender now the right to hold bitterness toward anyone and I will heal you.

*"Let all bitterness, wrath, anger, clamor and evil speaking be put away from you, with all malice."* (Ephesians 4:31)

Ask for forgiveness and I will forgive you. Forgive everyone who has hurt you. Make a list and confess your judgments against them and I will heal your hurting heart.

Do you question my voice? I assure you I was there when you were conceived, and I am making all things new. Spend time with me, and know it is not because of what you have done that you are saved, but it is because of what I have done and am doing.

*"For by grace you have been saved through faith, and that not of yourselves; it is the gift of God, not of works, lest anyone should boast."* (Ephesians 2:8-9)

Walk closely with me in your quiet time; begin to record my happenings and your diligence will be rewarded. I love you.

*"As the Father loved me, I also have loved you; abide in my love."* (John 15:9)

## This Country Is Not Free

Guard your heart and mind and remember the Alamo. I say this because this country will be overthrown and will no longer be united. This country is not free—it is full of chains:

The love of money,

The lust of the flesh, and

The pride of life.

Learn all you can from these instructions. As I speak, I am giving you increased wisdom as you have asked—wisdom beyond your years. Don't be discouraged by anything, but realize, I have fully encouraged you and carved out for you a place in this temporary world.

## To a Pastor and His Family

I am pleased with your willingness to serve me and those in your church family, but I say, go into the world and share these practices.

*"And he said to them, "Go into all the world and preach the gospel to every creature."* (Mark 16:15)

You are precious in my sight, each one, but you need to break out of your limited systems and seek and help save the lost, broken, and hurting.

*"For the Son of Man has come to seek and to save that which was lost."* (Luke 19:10)

Fear has kept you in isolation; now move beyond it and your faith will grow in increasing measure.

*"So we may boldly say: "The LORD is my helper; I will not fear. What can man do to me?"* (Hebrews 13:6)

You have built yourself a little bubble of safety, but I tell you, it is an illusion set up by legalism. It is my desire that you not be judging of others but walk in love and acceptance.

*"Do not speak evil of one another, brethren. He who speaks evil of a brother and judges his brother, speaks evil of the law and judges the law. But if you judge the law, you are not a doer of the law but a judge."* (James 4:11)

Learn to reach out to your community, embracing people who do not fit your pretenses. The time is short and fear is a mirage. I want you to move in a new faith, believing in my ability to provide beyond your limited understanding.

*"But without faith it is impossible to please him, for he who comes to God must believe that he is, and that he is a rewarder of those who diligently seek him."* (Hebrews 11:6)

I am the Lord your God; I can see what you cannot. I am disgusted by rote religious practices that are empty and fleeting. There is not a pat answer for the things of my Spirit; my answers vary depending on the details of each unique situation.

Continue to spend more time with me. Allow my love and acceptance to increase your understanding.

> *"Consider what I say, and may the Lord give you understanding in all things."* (2 Timothy 2:7)

I appreciate your service and obedience, but safety is in my protection, not in your protection for yourself.

> *"Be merciful to me, O God, be merciful to me! For my soul trusts in you; and in the shadow of your wings I will make my refuge."* (Psalm 57:1)

Don't be afraid any longer, for it counters every kind of faith, and faith is what I require. I want for all of you the very best possible outcome. My love is endless and my grace is abundant.

> *"And the grace of our Lord was exceedingly abundant, with faith and love which are in Christ Jesus."* (1 Timothy 1:14)

Think bigger,

Trust more, and

Renew yourself in the quiet time you spend with me.

> *"And do not be conformed to this world, but be transformed by the renewing of your mind, that you may prove what is that good and acceptable and perfect will of God."* (Romans 12:2)

Be willing to surrender your own ideas and ask me to show you my unlimited nature and your lives will be

Enhanced,

Pressed down, and

Pouring over.

*"Give and it will be given to you: good measure, pressed down, shaken together and running over will be put into your bosom. For with the same measure that you use, it will be measured back to you."* (Luke 6:38)

You cannot begin to understand the rewards of your individual surrender. Give up everything and follow me.

*"Then he said to them all, "If anyone desires to come after me, let him deny himself, and take up his cross daily, and follow me. In return you will have all of heaven to gain, even here on earth."* (Luke 9:23)

I do not speak to you now with any form of condemnation, but with love and compassion.

*"There is therefore now no condemnation to those who are in Christ Jesus, who do not walk according to the flesh, but according to the Spirit."* (Romans 8:1)

Reach out beyond your own walls and draw in

The cast down,

The broken, and

Rejected.

Then I will heal the hurting. Stop trying to appear to be perfect and invite imperfect, broken people into your care and you will see what it is really to serve me. I have not called you to create comfort; rather

I have called you to press through in battle as victors. Fight the good fight and mighty will be your reward.

> *"Fight the good fight of faith, lay hold on eternal life, to which you were also called and have confessed the good confession in the presence of many witnesses."* (1 Timothy 6:12)

Do you question my voice?

> *"Pilate therefore said to him, "Are you a king then?" Jesus answered, "You say rightly that I am a king. For this cause I was born and for this cause I have come into the world, that I should bear witness to the truth. Everyone who is of the truth hears my voice."* (John 18:37)

Hear me afresh and anew. My sheep hear my voice and a stranger's voice they will not follow.

> *"My sheep hear my voice, and I know them, and they follow me."* (John 10:27)

Bind the voice of the Stranger and begin to write down what I show you.

> *"And when he brings out his own sheep, he goes before them; and the sheep follow him, for they know his voice. Yet they will by no means follow a stranger, but will flee from him, for they do not know the voice of strangers."* (John 10:4-5)

You are about to embark on the great adventure as I have intended—to the full. Expose the darkness and learn how to battle in the Spirit.

> *"For we do not wrestle against flesh and blood, but against principalities, against powers, against the rulers of the darkness of this age, against spiritual hosts of wickedness in the heavenly places."* (Ephesians 6:12)

Use the power of testimonies or you will rob me of glory and the opportunity to build my church in faith.

> *"And they overcame him by the blood of the Lamb and by the word of their testimony, and they did not love their lives to the death."* (Revelation 12:11)

I am pleased with all of you and see you as precious. Seek me and you will find me when you seek me with all—and I mean, ALL your heart.

> *"And you will seek me and find me, when you search for me with all your heart."* (Jeremiah 29:13)

# April 17th

## I Watch Your Progress with Joy

It brings me great joy to watch your progress as you become accelerated in your ability to hear my voice. Know my heart of love; pour out what I give you, and overflow with the substance of heaven. Like raging rivers, I flow in the natural. Don't be afraid of any man, for all, great and small, require the same substance to live.

*"The fear of man brings a snare, but whoever trusts in the LORD shall be safe."* (Proverbs 29:25)

You are as mighty as any because of what I have done. Observe others' arrogance, but don't allow yourself to be filled with pride because I raise the humble up and exalt the lowly.

*"For whoever exalts himself will be humbled, and he who humbles himself will be exalted."* (Luke 14:11)

## No Reservation Needed

I will pour out splendor on those who come to me. It is never necessary to make a reservation with the Living God. Do you know that my word is alive, capable of setting free the hardest of captives?

*"The Spirit of the LORD is upon me, because he has anointed me to preach the gospel to the poor; he has sent me to heal the brokenhearted, to proclaim liberty to the captives and recovery of sight to the blind, to set at liberty those who are oppressed."* (Luke 4:18)

I see the world judging the outcasts, and I receive those rejected because of their brokenness. I draw them in with love and grace; I shower them with clothing of holiness. Their robes are not borrowed but given from heaven; they bestow the same generosity to others and experience joy.

*April 18th*

## A Word to a Pastor

I have been with you through many challenges and you are still standing. I will not abandon you now. We will break the back of Religious Pride together, and humility will raise up your ministry to new heights. I am preparing the feast, and we will celebrate together the new beginning. Don't let reduction fool you. I am adjusting the seats as musical chairs so the right foundation is in place to build upon. My vision for you is clear—trust me when I say I have made my plans and they are good. Remember that it is the struggle that makes one strong.

Where you've been is not important now; it is this present I give you. Focus on what is happening and bring every thought captive to determine its result.

> *"For the weapons of our warfare are not carnal but mighty in God for pulling down strongholds, casting down arguments and every high thing that exalts itself against the knowledge of God, bringing every thought into captivity to the obedience of Christ, and being ready to punish all disobedience when your obedience is fulfilled."*
> (2 Corinthians 10:4-6)

Don't hold on to anything that is not a piece of my puzzle—disregard any piece that does not belong or fit for I have given you my clear picture.

Restore the broken;

Bless the weak that resist your love;

Embrace the hurting, and

Walk in the light as I am in the light.

Put aside completely your own ambition and I will direct you with infinite wisdom. You are not at war with what can be seen, but you know you must fight in the Spirit the things of the Spirit.

> "Put on the whole armor of God, that you may be able to stand against the wiles of the devil. For we do not wrestle against flesh and blood, but against principalities, against powers, against the rulers of the darkness of this age, against spiritual hosts of wickedness in the heavenly places. Therefore take up the whole armor of God, that you may be able to withstand in the evil day, and having done all, to stand." (Ephesians 6:13-13)

This is a call to battle and you are being made a mighty warrior. Lay aside all forms of ego and worldly wisdom and ask for wisdom from heaven, and I will reward your request.

> "If any of you lacks wisdom, let him ask of God, who gives to all liberally and without reproach, and it will be given to him." (James 1:5)

Be not discouraged, for I go before you in Spirit and truth. I go with you in love and power. Mighty is your call and quick is my response to your asking.

## Spirit of Fear

I have not given you this assailing Spirit of Fear, but of love and power over it to have a sound mind.

> *"For God has not given us a spirit of fear, but of power and of love and of a sound mind."* (2 Timothy 1:7)

My peace is being released upon you. Joy is released in my Holy presence. Remember that I am with you. You will see breakthrough in your family—I am revealing myself to each member increasingly. I am answering your prayer; this will be your year of victory. You will learn more about the power of the tongue.

> *"Death and life are in the power of the tongue, and those who love it will eat its fruit."* (Proverbs 18:21)

More and more you will speak what has not yet happened as if it is—not to deceive yourself but to move in faith, believing for what has not yet come to pass.

## I Will Transform What You Give to Me

Hold onto me as I have held onto you; remember my promises to you. I will do exactly what I say; there is much I will do to use your unique testimony to share my miracles of healing and restoration. Be encouraged this day, for I bring you into a new season of victory. I will transform everything that you give to me—like changing every part on your collector auto—I desire to make all things new, I mean ALL things.

> *"Then He who sat on the throne said, "Behold, I make all things new." And He said to me, "Write, for these words are true and faithful."* (Revelation 21:5)

My blessing is upon you; in me you lack no good thing.

> *"The young lions lack and suffer hunger; but those who seek the LORD shall not lack any good thing."* (Psalm 34:10)

Speak the truth to every situation and you will release faith and disperse anxiety.

> *LORD, who may abide in your tabernacle? Who may dwell in your holy hill? He who walks uprightly and works righteousness and speaks the truth in his heart."* (Psalm 15:1-2)

I love you beyond your understanding.

# April 19th

## I Am Perfect Theology

*Lord, who should I give a word to today?*

I want to speak to YOU. I am bringing my churches together. I am preparing my beautiful bride to receive me. Many are imbalanced—far to the right or far to the left.

I am the pinnacle of perfect balance;

I am perfect theology;

I am perfect in deed.

## I Am Your Compass

Peace is powerful; it cannot be purchased, yet it is highly coveted. I am upon you; wear me well. I am your compass of true north. I guide you through extreme conditions and you are not deceived.

*"Do not be deceived, God is not mocked; for whatever a man sows, that he will also reap."* (Galatians 6:7)

*I saw myself standing on top of a mountain, hands outstretched like an eagle. The wind came and lifted me off the top of the mountain to observe other mountain peaks that God was also touching.*

Hear the frequency of my voice stirring in you that which is lifting. Spread out your arms like the eagle and soar upon my breath's wind, for my current will show you where to land. Here are my dynamics of simplicity:

*I saw clouds swirling, God's light shining upon them, and as the light increased, the motion of the protons increased. I saw a round center, like a yoke, with small particles swirling around it. The motion accelerated as the light continued to shine. I dive into the ocean and am launched from the water like a breaching whale.*

Soon—very soon, my ministry in you will be launched into orbit. I will be the center, drawing people toward my nucleolus. You are a magnetic proton repelling the electrons as my light accelerates their motion. I am a force beyond compare and you will move with me in mighty power, rooted in humility. Always point to me, for I am the one who chose you for this purpose.

Sit with me often as I continue to advance upon you. Submerge into my ocean and I will launch you out much farther than before. The angels catch your projection and fly you on to your next point of contact. Point toward the heavens in every good that is done, and I will keep you moving. Do not lose sight of this vision; it is your destiny.

## Your Mind is the Faculty of Learning

Be secure in your identity, for it is rooted in me. No one can tell you what you are not when I have told you what you are. Be renewed in your mind, for it is the faculty of learning and I want it sharp.

*"And do not be conformed to this world, but be transformed by the renewing of your mind, that you may prove what is that good and acceptable and perfect will of God."* (Romans 12:2)

Throw off anything that hinders, and rest only when I make you lie down.

*"Therefore we also, since we are surrounded by so great a cloud of witnesses, let us lay aside every weight, and the sin which so easily ensnares us, and let us run with endurance the race that is set before us looking unto Jesus, the author and finisher of our faith, who for the joy that was set before him endured the cross, despising the shame, and has sat down at the right hand of the throne of God."* (Hebrews 12:1-3)

Flow in the spirit as a melody and allow my never-ending song to dance upon the core of your mind where the seeds live.

*"Speaking to one another in psalms and hymns and spiritual songs, singing and making melody in your heart to the Lord, giving thanks always for all things to God the Father in the name of our Lord Jesus Christ."* (Ephesians 5:19-20)

## Activate My Blessing

Do in word and deed to activate my blessings so that you can be full of life.

*"And whatever you do in word or deed, do all in the name of the Lord Jesus, giving thanks to God the Father through Him."* (Colossians 3:17)

Lift my promise up and offer it back to become my blessing. Pull down the ripe fruit of my tree of goodness and share it, for there is plenty, and it is meant to be consumed. If it were set in storage, it would rot, so share it while it is in your reach. Pick up the pieces of fruit; they are clues like candles—the more you gather, the brighter the light. Bring me your full heart of many chambers and I will give you advanced design.

## Open Another Room

Exhilarating acceleration has opened another room; let's explore it together. You have sat there many times, but there is much you haven't noticed. I will adjust the lighting to highlight points of interest for the release of my purposed message.

A little adjustment,

    A little remodeling,

        A little redesign, and

            Behold—all things are new.

This room has no La-Z-Boy—

It is filled with diligence

    And is painted royal colors.

Its paintings are priceless,

    And its draperies are as white as snow.

The stars make up its ceiling,

    But beyond them is a place

Where all of heaven's singing

Can be heard in outer space.

Coming out of outer darkness,

You stand upon my light.

The picture that I'm painting,

You will clearly see tonight.

# April 20th

**Valued Quiet Time**

*Here I am, Lord. I've learned to enjoy my quiet time with you above all else.*

Remember my promise to guide and direct you when you seek me with all your heart.

> *"And you will seek me and find me, when you search for me with all your heart."* (Jeremiah 29:13)

Planter, you have collected my seeds as stories in your heart. Now you will begin sowing them into the hearts of those I show you, and I will bring the rain.

> *"He who continually goes forth weeping, Bearing seed for sowing, Shall doubtless come again with rejoicing, Bringing his sheaves with him."* (Leviticus 26:5)

**The Lord Speaks Through Me to a Pastor**

Thank you for your faithfulness to me.

*"May the LORD repay every man for his righteousness and his faithfulness."* (1 Samuel 26:23a)

I have delighted in you, even when you were just a small child—I was there.

*"He also brought me out into a broad place; He delivered me because He delighted in me."* (Psalm 18:19)

I have given you a new direction—one of promise, and I say move without encumbrance. I have set you free from your past completely to move you on to things present and things to come. Be not discouraged about anything, for I have brought new life. You will train my new recruits, and they will grow mighty in my kingdom. I have prepared you for such a time as this. Get ready—it's going to be exciting. You will reach into my fullness and I will pour out even more favor to lavish upon your efforts to serve me. I reward you with my peace and pour it out on your diligence.

*"Keep your heart with all diligence, for out of it spring the issues of life."* (Proverbs 4:23)

You have many questions, and I enjoy providing answers. You have sat at the bedside of the dying and have grieved with my saints, and I thank you with blessings from heaven. Be of good cheer, for I, the Lord your God, have equipped you to lead revival in this land. I have called you specifically, according to your gifting, and you will rise to answer my call. Your wife will be alongside you, and you will be increased in your ability to hear me. I give you heaven's blessings and say, jump into my raging river and you will not drown, for I am your redeemer and I am breathing life into deadness that it will live again. Put on your full armor and know that I will deliver you into victory as you have requested.

*"Put on the whole armor of God that you may be able to stand against the wiles of the devil."* (Ephesians 6:11)

In your quiet time with me, you will be made stronger still in your faith. I will raise up your family to do mighty kingdom work. They look to you for direction—I say point them back to me again. I wish to speak to each one, yet they don't all take time out just for me—if only they knew how I long to gather them up. My love is endless; there is no shortage in the land of plenty.

I have prepared your comings and goings, and I am pleased with your willingness to follow. I want more of your schedule; pencil in more time for me—there is much that needs to be done. You will be amazed by my design. I am developing from the supernatural to the natural what you have not yet conceived. Lay down your trophies—each one—and I will renew your soul. You will hear my voice in increasing measure, and I will add unto you more than what was expected.

*"Pilate therefore said to him, 'Are you a king then?' Jesus answered, 'You say rightly that I am a king. For this cause I was born and for this cause I have come into the world, that I should bear witness to the truth. Everyone who is of the truth hears my voice.'"* (John 18:37)

I love you beyond what you can possibly imagine, and I know you have done well, according to my purpose, but it is just the beginning— imagine that!

I will carry your burdens into glory, and I will cause you to become light in my fullness. Be ready to surrender all of your methodology and religious practices and I will give you new depths to explore. I pour out understanding, even in this message to you.

*"And he opened their understanding, that they might comprehend the scriptures."* (Luke 24:45)

Rest in what I tell you and live from victory. You are mighty in my kingdom, and I invite you to sit with me at my royal table. Come and enjoy my bounty. Release from my tree of goodness the blessings I have given. I do not tire of hearing you ask, but delight in every selfless request.

*"Be anxious for nothing, but in everything by prayer and supplication, with thanksgiving, let your requests be made known to God."* (Philippians 4:6)

I am eager to serve as a humble king, overseer of the kingdoms of this earth, but greater in power and might. Go and continue to serve me, sowing seeds that produce a bumper crop in the fertile soil of life. Offer unto me as I direct you. It will be clear as I reward your obedience. Test me again and see that I am always faithful. You have been prepared for greatness and will go to the ends of the earth with my message. Take your family with you for theirs is the kingdom of Heaven and lack is not possible in my house of many rooms—let us explore them together. I will be your tour guide and you will see more priceless treasure. I am breathing on your flame, and it burns hotter and brighter and bigger than before. Let me consume you—I tell you, you will not even smell like smoke.

# April 21st

**Know the Truth**

Peace comes from patience;

Patience comes from understanding;

Understanding comes from promise;

Promise comes from me, Jesus.

I come from the one who sent me—my Father.

He is in me and I am in him

That all will know the truth and be set free.

*"And you shall know the truth, and the truth shall make you free."*
(John 8:32)

Those who do not know me, do not know the truth, for how could you know the truth if you have never met me? Know me and you will have met the truth.

*"Then Jesus cried out, as He taught in the temple, saying, 'You both know me, and you know where I am from; and I have not come*

*of myself, but He who sent me is true, whom you do not know.'"* (John 7:28)

Live in me as I live in you and you will be free thus to experience the life, abundant in every possible way, with joy overflowing and love. Let me consume every thought. Allow my outpouring; speak into existence what you see in me and it will be manifest according to my will and purpose. I am carrying you to your destiny; cling to me as I move you along; hold on tightly to my promises and know that I will always keep them.

# April 22nd

*Today is Good Friday!*

## The Air You Breathe

The universe declares the voice that is my song.

My peace is like a melody blanket covering those who put it on.

Pull me up and wear me like surrounding comfort.

Take a bath in my love, living water surrounding skin.

Revive your youthful passions in my plethora of patience.

Shower yourself in the glory of my righteousness and you won't slip on anything unholy.

Walk on the clouds of your mind, stepping on clarity and understanding.

Jump and run with playfulness; Let me be your playground.

Rise up and hear the tones of my voice like the windy oceans.

Lie on my shores and absorb my goodness.

Roll around my salty beaches, and be filled with light that shines back on those who are drawn by it.

Jump on my waves of exhilaration, splashing onto the variations of majesty.

Send my waters flying so no one around you can stay dry.

Dive into my arms where the sun has a reason to shine!

Let me give light to your body until your body reflects my fullness.

Look on my jagged cliffs, erecting from my shores of solitude, and invite my seemingly subtle attributes to party, playfully—producing paradise.

Be surrounded by white, pure feathers and let them lift you over the monuments in victory.

Soar like the eagle that looks for a good place to land and let me be your nest.

Give birth to my purposes, and bring forth new life that will add to your team of duplication.

Let the stick of correction be your training center so not one will go untrained by it, but will follow you as you ride the strong and windy currents.

Flow through my skies, and let my breath dance around you like the angels I send to go with you.

Compelling is my countenance to fill to overflowing all who are thirsty, who shape themselves like an open glass trumpet; fingers stretched out to receive me.

Let me fill you with the sounds of birds that are enjoying the perfect day, not one of trillions that has not been counted.

Spring from me, like a diving board, into pools of everlasting, with restored imagination, bringing visions and dreams.

Let me be the air you breathe when your swim becomes airless or you feel like you can't breathe. Just gather my bubbles and they will revive your perceptions. Rise again to the surface, emerging like sunken treasure, and allow yourself to be spent so I can repay you.

## Hide In My Love

*This song was inspired by the poetic words given above.*

### Verse 1

The universe declares the voice that is my song;

My peace is like a blanket to those who put it on.

Shower in the glory of my righteousness,

So you won't slip on anything unholy.

### Chorus

Hide in my love, in the shelter of my wings;

Come fill this heart—with every good thing.

### Verse 2

Flow through my sky and let my breath dance around you:

Like the angels that I send to go with you.

Compelled by my countenance to fill to overflowing;

All who come and who are thirsty,

They will be filled with the fullness of truth.

### *Verse 3*

Shape yourself like an open glass trumpet,

Fingers stretched to the sky—oh Lord, to receive you.

I'll fill you with the sounds of birds enjoying the perfect day—

Restoring imagination and bringing visions and dreams.

Rise again to the surface, emerging like sunken treasure;

Allow yourself to be spent so I can repay you!

### *Bridge:*

My peace is filling the hungry;

My light is beaming in your soul.

My Spirit, flowing like a river,

Setting free everyone who knows.


## Good Friday Rap

### *Verse*

I come to your door like ebb and flow—

To share the love with seeds to sow.

At first yah say no, then yah beg for mo—

Rolling and filling like a pin on dough.

Go speaking the truth about whatcha know—

Things that are real all coming together, like a feather

The piece of a puzzle spread on a trestle—

What I lay down yah wanna pick up and guzzle.

There's no way to muzzle the truth, now bursting the seams;

I can't keep it inside when you're coming to me.

Yes it is! Yes it is!

Gonna find a way to praise my Lord—every day—every way!

Maybe you haven't arrived at this—

You think illusion is projecting a bliss,

But, pow! It hits you like a base drum rhythm;

Taking you back in time where Jesus came to knock your door.

Come to me—so much to show—

I wanna take you for a ride;

Invite me in and I'll come inside and

I'll sit with you and you will never be the same.

I want your sin and I'll take your pain—no more shame;

It's not a game—you'll never be the same.

Light the truth and truth is light;

Yah know the Devil's gonna put up a fight!

The victory's won; it's time to walk it out;

The heaven's cheer; time to shout no doubt!

Like a touchdown pass,

Prayers are heard from the back of the class,

Flowing like a mailman, drop in the sound;

Grabbing the message before it hits the ground.

Open it up—yah see your name on the page—

Open the door; free the bird from the cage.

***Chorus:***

Peace, flowing like a river—peace flowing; bringing life to me.

Dive in from the shore of self;

Don't bring your wealth—all you need is me to stay afloat—

Make a note—don't gloat.

Give me all the weight—let me carry the load;

Not sinking in the thoughts I'm thinking.

Eyes fixed so I can't be blinking.

I throw off the sin that's been sticking—no heavy drinking.

Cooling in the middle of a holy breeze,

Brought me to my knees.

## Forgiveness

Forgiveness is like taking a shower—the soap and water are endless. But when we get out and walk around and get dirty, we need to take another one. But remember, no one likes it when you use up all the hot water.

## My Love

My love is an ocean—

Dive in and let me consume you.

There are no sharks in my waters.

## Surrender to My Design

The created can never become their own creation. Since the beginning, my people have tried to draw up their own plans with broken pencils and then forget where the lead came from. I am still amused at watching them try to design their own lives, only to find that it wasn't what they thought apart from my beautiful picture. Your life is like a flower; your blossom is in proportion to your willingness to surrender.

## Friends

Friends should stick together like notes in a song—

Melodies and harmonies that all get along.

Labor and love is like a teeter-totter;

They are meant to be shared—

One pushes off, when the other gets scared.

**You Should Know**

It takes a lot of water to change the shape of a rock.

But with enough time and pressure, you can learn a lot.

Unless you're not watching the pattern of flow from the challenge you face—

By now you should know.

# April 23rd

**Hi, Lord! How's the Most High?**

Thank you for asking; I never tire of hearing you ask. When you turn your thoughts to me, I transform them into my ideas, then send them back to renew your mind. Do you know that I'm renewing your mind?

*"And do not be conformed to this world, but be transformed by the renewing of your mind, that you may prove what is that good and acceptable and perfect will of God."* (Romans 12:2)

Your sharp memory is going to astonish those who really know you. I am opening chambers of your mind that have never been used; creative areas of restored cells are firing up for the first time.

# April 25th

## Son of Jacob

Thank you for your obedience to me; the fruit you see is just a sample of what is to come to bring freedom to those I have touched through your desire to obey. Well done, Son of Jacob. I have prepared the ground. Press into me and allow my fullness to restore your whole family. I am producing patience and reviving the broken. I am the healer of the wounded soul. I am releasing heaven in you through what I have given. I see you giving away what I have given, and I am delighted. Great is your call and mighty is my ability to save. I send you on this mission perfectly equipped to carry out the assignment I have trusted you with, so rise up in your lowly posture and continue to exalt me. As you have spoken truth into so many, I speak truth into your destiny that many will know that I live.

> *"He who speaks truth declares righteousness, but a false witness, deceit."* (Proverbs 12:17)

# April 27th

## Brain Builders

*Certain words placed together can form exercises that strengthen brain cells. The Lord gives me rhyming words quite often so I can practice repetitious renderings which reach parts of my brain I am totally unaware of. Here's a sample:*

- Banter bricks, banter bricks, build them up high; no wall is too big for El Shaddai.

- Basic beauty is begotten beginning with brilliant simplicity.

- Bask in my banter blanket and become my billow of boldness.

- Become a member but have the eyes of the owner.

- Bento belongs beneath benevolence.

- Blessings become blossoms when properly placed.

- Centuries centurions centered on syntax.

- Climb into my class of discovery and collect my colostrums.

- Climb on my sunset and I'll take you around the world.

- Dance on distress and dissipate its dungeon.

- Giberson Gilbert's given to goodness.

- Give me Gustav and glory will be your gauntlet.

- Nursing nipples now nourish; natural nectar not needed nor nec essary now, Nathan.

- People ponder my principles but only prospectors produce my products.

- Pinnacle procedures prepare produce that prospers.

- Planets are plain without proper placement.

- Prepare pontification.

- Read Revelation and ready routines rerouted in revival.

- Right in front, riddles to rack your remembrance recalling retina to restored membrane.

- Run my rhythms through rhymes that represent restoration and reap readiness for road trip.

- Sow goodness and plenty will be your harvest.

- Tunics and toasters totally triturate.

# April 28th–May 2nd

## Road Trip

*I had been thinking that I'd like to take a road trip to Redding, California to visit the Bethel Church that I'd heard so many good things about. One morning, the Lord said he would like to take me on a journey. He said, "You will leave this weekend when you have $1,000 in savings and all your minimums are paid." I had $300—that's a $700 shortfall! That night, prompted by the Lord, a friend pulled into my driveway and handed me a check for the exact amount of $700. I was utterly amazed! I called my friend, Troi Cockayne, and said, "I guess we're going to Bethel." That weekend, we entered the adventure the Lord had planned for us. He gave us several assignments, and based on his instructions, we carried out each one. The following stories are but a sampling of our experience.*

## Heading South

*We headed south on I-5. Troi was driving and the Lord said to me, "I want you to stop at the next exit and pray for a woman who is wearing a sweatshirt. She has a pinched nerve in her lower back and I want to heal her."*

*"Hey, Troi, stop at the next exit—the Lord just said he wants to heal a woman of a pinched nerve in her lower back. She'll be wearing a sweatshirt."*

*"Are you kidding me?" he asked.*

*"Nope, that's what the Lord just said."*

*We took the next exit, which was for a rest area, and we saw a lady sitting on a blanket, and she was wearing a sweatshirt. We approached her and I said, "Sorry to bother you, ma'am, but we were driving down the freeway, and the Lord told me there was a woman at this exit, with a pinched nerve in her lower back, wearing a sweatshirt, and he wants to heal her. Is that you? Do you have a pinched nerve in your lower back?*

*She looked astonished, hesitated to respond, but then said, "Yes, I do. How do you know that?"*

*"Like I said, the Lord told me, and the good news is that he's about to heal you. The Lord loves you so much that he would send two perfect strangers off the freeway to come and pray for you. Is it okay if we pray for you?*

*"Yes," she said, "but people have been praying for me for four years and nothing has happened. I fell off a horse and was paralyzed from the neck down. I've regained some motion but have not been able to work because of it."*

*"That's okay—today's your day!" I laid my hands on her back and commanded it to be healed in the name of Jesus. She began to experience heat flowing into her back, and I said, "Your back is getting totally healed. He makes all things new—nothing shall be impossible for those who believe. In a few moments, I'll take my hands off your back and you will stand up and your back will be restored." I waited until I heard the Lord say, "It's*

*done." Then I said, "It's done." I took my hands off her back and said, "Try it out—do something you couldn't do before."*

*She reached down and put her palms to the ground and said, "Well, I couldn't do this." Then she reached up with her arms and fingers stretched to the heavens and burst into tears, then laughed, saying, "I'm healed!" She started dancing with joy.*

*Troi and I stood in total amazement at what the Lord had just done. We all laughed together, praising and thanking God.*

## Vista Point

*As we continued south, the Lord said to pull off one mile ahead at the Vista Point lookout. We did. No one was there. I saw a vision of a motor home pulling up behind us, and sure enough, just then a motor home pulled up behind us. The Lord said, "This is it," followed by, "Lower back; left knee." A man got out of his vehicle and came around the side of it. I got out of the car and hollered over, "Hi, there! Do you have a problem with lower back pain?"*

*He said, "Yes, and so does my wife."*

*"And is your right knee giving you trouble?"*

*"Why, yes."*

*"Well, I believe God wants me to pray for you. Would that be okay?"*

*"Come on around."*

*Troi joined us and the gentleman introduced us to his wife. I asked whether the family could come out and join us in the prayer. They did and the Lord instructed me to ask the children to lay hands on their father while Troi and I prayed. I said something like, "Back be restored in Jesus' name: every cell, every muscle, every joint and tendon—come into perfect alignment right now. Thank you, Lord, for healing this back." The Lord brought healing through the children as we agreed in faith. We then prayed for the father's right knee and Troi led the children in prayer for his wife. Again, the Lord brought his miracles.*

*I prophesied to the family a word the Lord was forming in my Spirit: I could see that money had been taken from their family and I was to tell them that the Lord was going to give it back. They agreed, saying there had been a real estate deal that had gone bad because of greed, and they were suffering financially at the loss of their retirement funds.*

*We were interrupted by the children seeing smoke coming from inside the motor home. Their father quickly began to search for the origin, inside then out. He opened a side panel and two small flames were exposed on two separate wires—one on the right and one on the left—above the gas line. We blew the flames out and when the smoke stopped, the realization hit us all that had they not pulled over when they did, the motor home could have exploded.*

## At the Chevron Station near Mt. Shasta

*We filled the tank at a Chevron station the Lord guided us to. He told me to talk to a woman worker in the back room. I asked the clerk whether there was a woman in the back room. He said there was and I asked to speak to her. He guided me to the back and introduced me to the woman. I shared with her that the Lord wanted her to sing again. She looked at me with big eyes, as if her heart had just skipped a beat, and in her silence, I said, "You were discouraged about your singing, so you stopped, but the Lord gave you a voice and he longs to hear it." She was stunned. I was made aware that she had back pain, and I asked her whether she would like prayer for it. "Yes," she said. I prayed and the Lord simply healed her.*

*Troi came into the gas station and told me a young man was in the parking lot who had a problem with his back and needed prayer. We prayed and God took the pain away immediately. The young man got quiet, looked around, and said, "Guys, I've got to tell you something. Earlier this morning, my Christian mother told me that someone would come up to me today, and when he did, I was going to know that God exists." His eyes were full of tears and amazement.*

## Bethel Church

Bethel's mission is REVIVAL…the personal, regional, and global expansion of God's kingdom through his manifest presence.

## Speak to the Lady

*On the return trip, driving North on I-5, the Lord told us to take the next exit. He proceeded to guide us to a winery where he highlighted a woman behind the counter and said to me, "Speak to the lady behind the counter and tell her this":*

I want you to know that I speak, and I desire that you will hear me as I speak to you now. You will break out of unbelief as you press into me, for I am the Lord your God, maker of heaven and earth. Your destiny is in my hands, and I release its fullness. You have been richly blessed, and can you imagine that it's just the beginning?

My love is like a melody blanket—put me on and wear my perfect peace. Let your journey be enriched by the fullness of my open heaven, and let resurrection become your new song. My love for you is endless; my grace on your family is abounding. Sing with the fullness of my kingdom and usher in my bounty. I want you to live astounded.

Do you not know that you have tapped into my goodness? Now drink deep.

Your blossom will be proportionate to your surrender. I am filling you with an increased measure, and you are going to be amazed. Thank you for praying for my people. Thank you for the prayer of restoration over your family. I have heard you, daughter, and I am answering your requests. I saw you from the foundation of the establishment of the earth, and I smile hugely when I look at your face. You glow with my holiness. You bless me. The heavens join your worship and I will reveal my kingdom to you.

*This lady seemed to be in total shock after hearing this word and later sent me an email expressing her gratefulness, saying that a normal day at the winery was interrupted by an amazing encounter with God—one that has totally changed her life.*

## Speak to the Man

*A gentleman was sitting at the counter of the same winery and I sat down next to him to sample the wines. The Lord started speaking to me about this man. I said to him something like, "You know, the Lord talks to me and he's speaking about you right now. Would you like me to write it down and give it to you?" He said, "Sure."*

Your life is like a fine wine—I have given you the perfect mixture of goodness. You have enjoyed the finer things, and I see your heart and it is beautiful. I love the love that you share with your family. You have invested in college, but the things I'm investing in you are much more valuable. I have given you supernatural wisdom and ability to discern truth. I delight in your inquisition. Your need to figure out why things work the way they work was given to you by me.

Do not worry about your mother for she is with me. Your father, who has gone before, enjoys the benefits of paradise. I want you to rely on my Holy Spirit to hear—rely on my voice and not on your own knowledge. Your intelligence is extreme, but do not forget where it came from. You have worked hard and have enjoyed the fruits of your labor, but I fashioned the mind, the faculty of remembrance.

The wounds of the soul are created by sin and you know that sin needs a savior. I do not condemn you, but delight in every discovery as I walk with you. My desire is that you would hear me in increasing measure. Your soul is made up of three parts: mind, will, and emotions. I am the door; walk through me. My kingdom is at hand and I invite you to my royal table.

Shower your wife with my love. A mighty harvest is a result of the seeds you have sown. And as I have told you, I continue to bring rain. I see you as a tree rooted deep in the fertile soil, giving shelter to all bold enough to gather under your shade. Drop the fruit from your branches and allow yourself to be broken for my name's sake, for I am He, sent from heaven that you would be redeemed in my purpose to be a blessing—to show others to give as I have given. You, mighty son of Jacob, have the favor of kings.

You have aged well; you have maintained youthfulness in your perceptions. You have exercised my likeness. I am the healer of all your pain. I have paid the price that your right leg would be restored, that you would walk with newness on earth as it is in heaven. Spend more time with me alone; there is much I have to say. Receive my love for I have brought you great comfort, for I am the mighty comforter; greater things will you do than these. Finish well the race that I have charted and leave behind your legacy of love.

## Lake Shasta

The Lord told me to take the Lake Shasta exit and we did. I sat on the dock with my feet in the water and reflected on the goodness of the Lord. I was utterly amazed beyond my wildest expectations that He is increasingly better than what I ever imagined. Lord what would you like to say to me?

I have waited so long for you to get to this point of total surrender to me, and I am with you as I have revealed, and I will continue to bring supernatural encounters, visions, signs and wonders, and miracles rooted deep from my heart of love. You have believed and now have seen; you have tasted my feast, and I will keep the food of heaven replenished for the nourishment of your soul. I tell you that you are being celebrated by the angels in heaven as you walk by faith—not by sight. I have given you my eyes to see as you have asked and nothing—I said nothing—shall be impossible for you.

I am surrounding your world with the blanket of my melodies, and I will shake it out to fan the flame of revival. Be being filled with my radiance that your light will reflect the glory of my father. Remember, I am the Lord your God, maker of heaven and earth—the one who sends and the one who speaks life to the hopeless. My creation power is upon your tongue, so speak my song and it will be sung. Do not lose sight of your destination, but savor each moment of this divine journey because I have fully adopted you into my kingdom. You are my son and you can ask me for anything you like. My will is to bless you—just remember to keep "things" simply as "things," and don't ever lose sight of me as your focus and you will be set in all that I have established.

*The lake was clear and still yet suddenly a floating piece of wood hit my feet. It looked just like the base of a cross. I gathered it with my feet and cen-*

*tered it. I saw myself being laid down as a sacrifice for him, being reminded that he freed me in this way.*

This wood I have sent you is a reminder to you to be a sacrifice to my people, just as I have sacrificed myself for you. Because of my systems of resurrection, you cannot be destroyed. Cling to the work that was finished at the cross, and stretch your hands toward your destiny, and I will move you toward it like a freight train.

*At that very moment a train blew its chilling bellow as if to confirm the Lord's voice. The timing was almost unbelievable, but I do believe and delight in the demonstrations of my Savior.*

> *"I have glorified you on the earth. I have finished the work which you have given me to do. And now, O Father, glorify me together with yourself, with the glory which I had with you before the world was."*
> (John 17:4-5)

Become my message of love. Give as I have given and I have approved. Move into my destiny of greatness. Release the holy heavens.

Sanctify,

   Redeem in my name,

      Restore,

         Pursue,

            Declare,

               Decree,

                  Proclaim,

Speak into existence what has not been seen, and I tell you, it will materialize. The skies obey me, and they hear your voice for I speak through you. Don't be alarmed; this is not blasphemy—it is kingdom reality. My kingdom has been established in you as it is in heaven; therefore, I say to you again, it has no limitation. Walk in this truth and all will see that the knowledge of the truth needs to become a life of faith, walking as you have just experienced. The Destroyer has no access to what you have walked out [acted in obedience, by faith] and on this foundation, it cannot be destroyed.

Rise up my mighty melody; rise up my mighty servant; do as I have done and now great is your reward. You could not be more blessed or highly favored—now act like it and you will see for yourself what I have said. Do you know the height or the depth of my love?

> *"For I am persuaded that neither death nor life, nor angels nor principalities nor powers, nor things present nor things to come, nor height nor depth, nor any other created thing, shall be able to separate us from the love of God which is in Christ Jesus our Lord."*
> (Romans 8:38-39)

Can you imagine infinity? Let's go on a ride. I release upon you the fullness of my faithful family, and I stamp you with my golden seal—

Approved,

Set free,

Redeemed,

Sanctified,

Holy,

Heaven bound.

Halleluiah! Halleluiah!

## A Vision of Heaven

These are my angels singing Halleluiah, praising me in the throne room of righteousness. As I showed you, gold dust swirls my kingdom and it does not have need of sweeping. What is clean cannot be cleaned; what is perfect cannot be destroyed.

Be now all that I have intended; open your hands and release the outbreak of my goodness. There will be no dry bones, but milk and honey flowing from heavenly balm. Bring my gifts into the storehouse of plenty, for I have given you the key. The supply is endless, so give away as much as you like, and it will never ever, ever, ever, ever run out. Peace be with you always, forever and ever and ever. Amen.

May 2011

# May 1st

## Your Identity Is in Me

I want you to hear this message because your identity is in me, rooted in royalty. You don't need to prove yourself worthy; I have made you worthy—

Sanctified,

   Holy,

      Redeemed, and

         Saved into my royal priesthood.

Walk now—not selling *yourself* any more, but carrying the flavor, smell, and favor of the most high—walking not in pride, but full humility. Be lifted high that the kingdom of God through Jesus Christ will be glorified.

## Sit on My Train

Shekhinah, shalom, super—not natural but naturally super, above what is seen by the common—I want you to sit on my train like the angels and join the choirs of heaven in their splendor. I have carried you in my arms and brought your destiny to your feet, and now I set you down to fulfill what has been given you from the kingdom of Heaven.

Are you seeing?

Are you hearing?

Are you believing?

Of course, I know the answer, but I ask the questions so you can answer them within yourself—within the deepest chambers of your heart where my treasure lives.

## Walk in My Rest

At the bottom of the river of humility is where the water is. Peaceful pastures prepared for rest wait for you to come lie down.

*"He makes me to lie down in green pastures; He leads me beside the still waters."* (Psalm 23:2)

Walk in my rest and be not anxious, for all that you need has been provided.

*"Be anxious for nothing, but in everything by prayer and supplication, with thanksgiving, let your requests be made known to God; and the peace of God, which surpasses all understanding, will guard your hearts and minds through Christ Jesus."* (Philippians 4:6-7)

To increase your blessings of resources released, release what has already been given. I love to remind you of the ways of my kingdom. I increase you as you give; I cannot be out-given. I know you know this, but—

*"Give and it will be given to you: good measure, pressed down, shaken together, and running over will be put into your bosom. For*

*with the same measure that you use, it will be measured back to you."*
(Luke 6:38)

I saw a vision of people coming off the Mountain of Pride and getting on to the Train of Humility. The train was effortlessly taking them to the top of the mountain. Others said, "I don't need to get on that train; I can walk on my own and I'll get there faster. With so much more effort they climbed, wore out their strength, and never did make it to the top.

*"Humble yourselves in the sight of the Lord, and he will lift you up."*
(James 4:10)

# May 6th

## I Have Unlocked the Doors

My Word is a lamp onto your feet; a life-giving source to all who are weak.

> *"Your word is a lamp to my feet and a light to my path."* (Psalm 119:105)

I will pour out on the hungry with bread of life to nourish necessity. Do you know I am with you now? Do you know I have made a way for you to have full access to my abundance? I have unlocked the doors—walk through the chambers of destiny—and do not deny my design. When I raise you up, it's a call to glorify. My goodness is the fruit you enjoy.

> *"But the fruit of the Spirit is love, joy, peace, longsuffering, kindness, goodness, faithfulness, gentleness, self-control. Against such there is no law."* (Galatians 5:22-23)

## I Am the One Who Duplicates

Enter into my courts with praise; love those who do not know love.

*"Enter into His gates with thanksgiving, And into His courts with praise. Be thankful to Him, and bless His name."* (Psalm 100:4)

Give to those who have need, and bathe in my holiness so that righteousness abounds. Sing to me as the angels join you; lead my people in the ways of praise. Give my measure to all who are hungry and they too will be filled. Paradise beckons the bold in me.

Be bold and meek,

Humble and ready,

Carefree but not careless.

See my ways and do as you see,

For I am the one who duplicates.

This is a pinnacle moment, and I have gone before you to establish what must come to pass for greatness to be attained. Be optimistic, for I have optimized your opportunities.

## Give Me More Time

Be aware of what moves around you and take the time to rest and reflect.

*"Let us therefore be diligent to enter that rest, lest anyone fall according to the same example of disobedience."* (Hebrews 4:11)

I will give you recharged restoration and livelihood. Loving kindness and mercies have come to visit you as you give me more time.

*"Oh, give thanks to the LORD, for he is good! For his mercy endures forever."* (Psalm 136:1)

This is your very best investment; it will pay the very greatest returns.

Can you see where we are going?

Do you know what I'm calling you to do?

Magnify the magnificent; chart the challenge for the children. I wish to speak to everyone and you will share:

How to listen and activate;

How to restore and liberate;

How to receive the fullness of my kingdom now—

On earth as it is in heaven.

# May 7th

## Nothing Shall Be Impossible

I want you to remember that when you walk with me, you cannot lose; there is no battle too great for us. I will conquer every army that tries to rise against my call.

> *"And I looked, and behold, a white horse. He who sat on it had a bow; and a crown was given to him, and he went out conquering and to conquer."* (Revelation 6:2)

I have caused your footsteps to become firm in the foundations of faith.

> *"Uphold my steps in your paths that my footsteps may not slip."* (Psalm 17:5)

Fire from heaven goes before you to burn away the illusions of fear and to light up every spirit that stands against you as you walk with me.

> *"He performs great signs, so that he even makes fire come down from heaven on the earth in the sight of men."* (Revelation 13:13)

You have received kingdom confidence, and I am revealing my strategies to you, one by one. Nothing shall be impossible.

*"For with God nothing will be impossible."* (Luke 1:37)

## I Delight in Your Love Songs

Continue to rise up, my son, and let my train of humility take you to the top of the mountain. Dance on the mountaintop and sing your praises, for I delight in your love songs to me. They are as water to the thirsty, bringing life and goodness.

> *"Let them praise his name with the dance; Let them sing praises to him with the timbrel and harp."* (Psalm 149:3)

Stay close and learn from me, for I am happy to teach you everything you'll need.

## The Harvest

"The sower sows and the gatherer gathers, but blessed is he who gathers what he has sown, for he sees both the planting and the harvest, then duplicates himself in more fields of plenty and the product comes back to repay him.

> *"The sower sows the word."* (Mark 4:14)

> *"He who gathers in summer is a wise son; He who sleeps in harvest is a son who causes shame."* (Proverbs 10:5)

The farmer who teaches his methods of success gives away my kingdom, and as a result, more glory is celebrated in heaven. The hungry ground is the best soil to plant seed in, for it is set to absorb. Absorption is proportionate to the level of hunger. When water sits on hard, dry ground, it sits on top until the moisture dampens its hard crust. I want to saturate the lives of those who have tasted and see, and those who will allow my help. Pride resists me, but I am eager to help those who will find the need for it.

*"Blessed are those who hunger and thirst for righteousness, for they shall be filled."* (Matthew 5:6)

When trees are planted they must be rooted in good soil—moist, not dry. Deep roots can occur and deep roots are what produce the most growth.

*"He shall be like a tree planted by the rivers of water, that brings forth its fruit in its season, whose leaf also shall not wither; and whatever he does shall prosper."* (Psalm 1:3)

The soil in you does not like to be churned, but churning is part of preparation to plant, and planting is my process of bringing forth life, rooted in fertile soil and filled to the top edge, not above the soil line.

*"Does the plowman keep plowing all day to sow? Does he keep turning his soil and breaking the clods?"* (Isaiah 28:24)

The plants will flourish with the right mixture of water and light. You have my water and I give you the right amount of light—now grow to bring forth a harvest that is astounding. Your tree will bring forth seed that brings many more trees under the shade of your branches, and these can be transplanted to bring about my mission. Keep planting and don't worry about credit. Just sow and harvest—what you see you will reap.

*"Do you not say, 'There are still four months and then comes the harvest'? Behold, I say to you, lift up your eyes and look at the fields, for they are already white for harvest!"* (John 4:35)

## Hell Is the Result of Sin

I am rewiring your retina responders so they can see in the Spirit. Not everyone could handle what I'm about to show you. I do not wish hell on anyone, yet hell is the result of sin. This is why I came to offer my son Jesus to bridge the gap in freedom from darkness and death.

The Lord showed me hell. It was dark and dangerous—-the only light coming was from fires burning the captives. The Devil appeared as a big torturous giant demon with large horns on his head and tense jaws. Captives in dripping, cavernous caves were being whipped and slapped around while chains clattered. Confusion and fear danced about the wicked evildoers while the Devil laughed and mocked. Why do you show me this, Lord?

I want you to save people from seeing it for real. Hell is a choice, born of ignorance—it is not my will for any to go there.

> *"The Lord is not slack concerning his promise, as some count slackness, but is longsuffering toward us, not willing that any should perish but that all should come to repentance."* (2 Peter 3:9)

> *"But I will show you whom you should fear: Fear him who, after he has killed, has power to cast into hell; yes, I say to you, fear him!"* (Luke 12:5)

Stay sharp and help save the lost. Salvation is upon your lips and danger will rise against you, but I have placed a force field of protection around you and your family. Lift up your hands and release my kingdom on the captives. Pour out my Holy Spirit by asking it to fall.

> *"While Peter was still speaking these words, the Holy Spirit fell upon all those who heard the word."* (Acts 10:44)

# May 8th

**My Love Drives the Universe**

Do you see how much I am doing and showing? I tell you it's just the beginning! You are in bloom and astounding will be the result of my life in you. You are moving according to my plan and design; press on and recall my miracles motivated by love. My love is the force that drives the universe; it's what sends stars flying across the sky; it cannot be shaken and will never be defeated.

> *"Behold what manner of love the Father has bestowed on us, that we should be called children of God! Therefore the world does not know us, because it did not know Him."* (1 John 3:1)

You have it, and now I commission you to share its fullness—go and make disciples of men; bring them up in the knowledge of me; help them by showing them how to access my kingdom power. Give yourself to them and observe their growing dependence on me and you will be as I intended.

> *"Go therefore and make disciples of all the nations, baptizing them in the name of the Father and of the Son and of the Holy Spirit."* (Matthew 28:19)

## Total Surrender

Peace is your melody blanket; love is the river I have set to flow through you. Guard your mind, guard your heart, shine for me, and reflect my light for many have not seen it.

> *"And the peace of God, which surpasses all understanding, will guard your hearts and minds through Christ Jesus."* (Philippians 4:7)

You're about to encounter a new kind of wonderful—

Embrace it!

Spring from it!

Dive into it!

Let nothing keep you from it! Becoming Christ-like is a process that is intended to be both trying and triumphant. Subjecting yourself in total surrender takes faith and trust and even trials of refinement. Blessing is a natural part of obedience and obedience is learned through discipline, thus producing disciples.

> *"For as by one man's disobedience many were made sinners, so also by one man's obedience many will be made righteous."* (Romans 5:19)

## Make Disciples of Men

Again, I say that I want you to make disciples of men. My purpose for you is the purpose of my father who sent me. Grab hold of my goodness and go gather what has already been seasoned. Bring each one who hungers into my throne room that he will be more than satisfied, jumping with gladness, full of joy and laughter. Give to those who are thirsty and splash upon their dry ground.

*"For I will pour water on him who is thirsty, and floods on the dry ground; I will pour my Spirit on your descendants, and my blessing on your offspring."* (Isaiah 44:3)

Let peace sooth the tormented and blanket the defeated.

# May 11th

## Start Again When You Fail

When you fail, dust off and start again, for everyone has room to grow. Remember that what I am preparing has great importance, and your kingdom call is kingdom come, so be alert and stay in balance with my leading. *Vaminos!* Get going and I will bless you. Believing it is easy makes it so; believing it is too hard makes things seem hard, so carry on with charisma and conquer constancy.

*"For my yoke is easy and my burden is light."* (Matthew 11:30)

## The Rock of the Harbor

I am preparing, through you, a church that will capture the fullness I have intended. The building will be as you have imagined: simple, square, and contemporary. This church will create a culture of all that I am—it will be called "The Rock of the Harbor." My Spirit will linger there and be full. I will instruct you and your leaders and great will be the harvest. You will train up leaders who will reach to the corners of the earth. My love will blanket those who come and many will sit with me, speechless.

All that I am and all that I do is from love, and love will be your theme—my love. You get it, and then I want you to give it away outrageously. Do not be afraid; I am bringing a mighty support group that will be with the twelve leaders who will share the privilege of bringing the message of a rotating pulpit. You will have everything needed from heaven to ignite a movement of my Spirit. I will add unto you every good and perfect gift. Get in order what I show you, and remember, just one step at a time.

*May 12-16th*

## Mexico Mission Trip

*I wasn't planning to go to Mexico this year, but I was open to the Lord's will. During the Sunday service at Chapel Hill,[1] it was announced there were two pre-paid places open for anyone wanting to go on the Men's Mexico Mission Trip. I almost jumped out of my seat at the Holy Spirit's prompting. That is how it was that I joined seventy men, donned with matching T-shirts, to board a jetliner in Seattle en route to San Diego where we would later load into vans for the trek into Tecate, a small city in Baja California, Mexico. Our goals were to build seven houses for pre-selected families, in partnership with Armor Ministries, and to build friendships and the faith of those we were going to serve.*

## Words to a Team Member

*I was sitting next to another team member on the plane when the Holy Spirit prompted me to deliver the following message to him.*

I am your provision. We have come so far together. I see your grief for your son, and I tell you the truth, he is in my hand. I will answer your request. I hear all your prayers, and you are so precious to me. I have

---

1  Chapel Hill Presbyterian Church in Gig Harbor, Washington.

approved you as a member of my royal family, and I have invited you to sit with me at my royal banquet. Give me more time alone. You are ready to enter a new season. I have prepared leadership in you since the foundations of the earth. I see you sitting with me, wondering how I will direct you this time.

Do not give into the Spirit of Fear, for it has been conquered by my perfect love and the work of the cross. I delight in your willingness to sow seeds of hope into the hopeless, and I see you caring for the least of these, and I say, "Well done, my faithful servant." Blessed are those who come in behind you, for you have made a way for their progression. I will equip you with every good thing. All of heaven will be open above you; nothing shall be impossible for you. You are mighty in my sight and the adventure has been perfectly planned. Blessed are those who come to me, for I am the Lord your God, maker of heaven and earth.

Craft with me what I have shown you and get your thoughts in order. I have called your steps—one by one. Move in faith and be bold, for heaven is on your lips. Speak into existence that which has not yet come to pass, and I tell you, it will be done according to my will and purpose. You are so important and special to me. I have filled you with a sensitive heart to pour out on the helpless. Let the broken horses come and surrender to my fullness, and see whether I do not pour out a blessing that cannot be contained. Ready your team for greatness and release my heart of love. You have my hands that the sick will be made well; let my mercy motivate your prayers to heal. Sit with me often and ready your pen for there is much to do. Enter my rest and work from it and you will not tire of serving. Thank you for responding to my call, Son of David. You are mighty in my eyes!

## Another Message

*While waiting for the luggage to roll, in the San Diego terminal, I was given yet another message for a team member.*

You are a beacon of my light and love; I am pleased with your willingness to serve my people. There is so much I want to show you about my kingdom here on earth as it is in heaven. I have made you to reflect my glory. It is I—the Lord your God, maker of heaven and earth, founder of foundations of faith. Believe me when I tell you that you haven't seen anything yet; what I am preparing to release inside of you is majesty that mirrors my melodies.

You are a speaker with a voice of victory. Give way to my fullness; be astounded by my love and mercy, for you have tasted and you have seen. Abounding joy is released upon you. Don't be so hard on yourself— you have been made humorous, so laugh and release my kingdom of faith and love in the face of fear. The heavens join your song, inspired by me. Prepare yourself and hear me speak. I have given you the keys to my kingdom; now access the resources therein, and tap the storehouse of plenty. I tell you the truth; nothing shall be impossible for you as you surrender every thought and walk with me.

My hand is upon your family; my provisions have funded your call. I am your security blanket; wrap me around you and lack no good thing. Lead this generation with bold humility and what has been promised to you will come to pass. You are mighty in my kingdom and could do nothing to be more approved by me. I love and accept you just the way you are, and I tell you that life as you know it is about to get very exciting.

Spend more time with me alone—there is much I want to say to you. Bind the voice of the stranger and let me speak to your soul. Sit with me and see whether I do not give you all you need for the journey that lies ahead. Press into me like never before and allow my release. I am adjusting your limited ideas to match my limitless realities.

Your songs will be celebrated;

Your life is my legacy;

You are enjoying my adventures; and

I have charted your steps.

Be teachable and allow my full direction. Bring your ideas before me and I'll give them back to you, denied or approved. Be careful not to adopt the ways of man. My son, Jesus, is perfect theology—if he does it, I want you to do it.

What if there is more than you have seen?

What if I'm greater than you ever imagined?

Get ready—life has only just begun!

## Sitting by the Fire

*We have settled in, met the local people, and have started building. Now we sit in a circle around the fire and I realize that we are not here only to build houses, but to bridge a gap between two cultures. Many miracles have already occurred to show us that the kingdom of Heaven is with us— kingdom reality has a way of breaking through the walls of unbelief and removing the barriers of limited thinking. The grace of God can truly flow through a submitted vessel and that's what we are. The Holy Spirit inter-*

*rupted my reverie with a word from himself to the men gathered around the fire that night.*

I love you with depths beyond what you are able to understand. Each one of you matters much to me. Your willingness to serve me by serving others is a selfless act of surrender. Oh, how I long for more acts of surrender to become a daily part of your life. I am the Lord your God, maker of heaven and earth. Take heed and know that I am with you even in the smallest acts of kindness; I delight in you.

The more you surrender, the more I surround. The more you press in, the more I equip you to press on. I tell you, the kingdom of Heaven is at hand; your harvest will be proportionate to the seed you sow. Be on guard for the thoughts that compete in your mind with my will and focus on the pure and lovely; and then, my peace will be as a blanket for your soul. Keep your eyes fixed on my design and great will be your reward, on earth as it is in heaven. Grow in boldness and do not be ashamed, for I have cancelled the debt of sin.

Now walk in freedom from your past and allow my fullness. Do not be ashamed to speak about me, for I am life to the lifeless. I offer freedom and abounding joy, abundance in every way. Learn of me and give me your burdens. Pull my promises close and cling to my purpose, for I have made you beautiful.

> *"He has made everything beautiful in its time. Also he has put eternity in their hearts, except that no one can find out the work that God does from beginning to end."* (Ecclesiastes 3:11)

## Church with the Locals

*It was Saturday in Tecate and some locals were walking past our work site. I was prompted to ask when the church service started and what building it was held in. One of the men pointed to a building. I tapped my watch to signify, "What time?" and one said, "Now!" Since we had not yet had our lunch break, I said to the guys, "Hey, let's do church with the locals." The Lord told me to grab a couple of my CDs, my second album titled,* Turn Around. *I thought this was a strange request since these people could not speak English.*

*We walked into the church and the band was already playing. All heads turned toward us as if this were a very unusual occasion—a group of seven gringos walking in with no invitation. The Lord told me to give one of my CDs to a woman walking by, and I did without a thought. We began to enter into worship, trying to sing Spanish the best we could. The presence of God was like a pleasing aroma in this simple little church built along the dusty hills of this small town.*

*Soon, I was asked by the pastor to come forward to sing with the worship band. I didn't know it at the time, but the woman I gave the CD to was the pastor's wife, and she had given him the CD. I came forward, a band member slung a guitar over my head, and I sang a couple of songs I had written, one especially for the people of Tecate. When I finished singing, they sprang to their feet, exploding with enthusiastic cheers. I started speaking while someone ran for an interpreter. Later, I gave him the other CD, and of course, he could speak English. I was able to tell this small group that we came to build houses, but more importantly, we came to show Christ's love. At the close, they joyfully gathered around us and invited us to join them for a meal, but we had to get back to work!*

## Sunday in Tecate

*The Lord spoke this to me in the morning…*

This is the final day of your trip, but the beginning of all things new. I have given you a supernatural understanding to know and follow my Holy Spirit. Be ready to drop your own plans when I lead you to follow mine. Great new adventures are around the corner, and I will enjoy watching you explore them, one by one. I delight in your reactions, opening the gifts I have wrapped just for you, much like you enjoy your own children's discoveries. I see you embracing life as I have intended, and I tell you that I am pleased. I know once again your level of gratitude has grown, and this is the thankfulness I require and delight in.

When you go back home, one slight change I would ask of you is that you talk less and listen more. Give yourself to my call and release the secrets of my kingdom. Be on guard for those who try to discredit you; walk blameless and always allow my direction. I will give you specific instructions, and you will listen and obey. Do not attempt to defend yourself; I am your defender.

Be loving and walk your talk of freedom, knowing I have made you strong. Paradise is on your lips. I have anointed you for such a time as this. Do not be afraid of anyone great, for you are great in my eyes. Thank you for loving my people. Blessings fall down upon you now and for evermore until the day I call you home to join the songs of heaven.

## You Are Mighty

*Gathered around the fire pit in the center of our portable tent city, the men were rehearsing the happenings of our adventure. We had accomplished our goals. Seven very happy families were moving into their newly-built, two-room homes, and we also had erected a larger structure to house a church. Months of careful planning will reap a harvest—how much? We might never know, but there is satisfaction in the assurance that we did our best. Soon we would start packing up and the trip would become only a memory, but the lessons the Lord had instilled in us would live on, creating a foundation for other ventures of faith. The Lord pressed a message on my heart for another team member, and I took a few minutes to capture it. This is what he said:*

You are mighty in my eyes. I see you sitting in my presence and delight in your ability to lead my people. You are as a strong tower in the rubble of wayward thinking.

*"The name of the LORD is a strong tower; the righteous run to it and are safe."* (Proverbs 18:10)

I have made you this way. I am the Lord your God, maker of heaven and earth, designer of your destiny. Press into me and increase in your ability to hear, for what I am planning for you is very exciting. I will reveal it in stages. I will pour out increased favor. Nothing, I say nothing, shall be impossible for you, my servant.

*"For with God nothing will be impossible."* (Luke 1:37)

Be on guard against wrongful judgments. Walk close to me in understanding and you will see my fullness. Restore the broken; lead the weak and strong, knowing that each one is very important to me. Surrender every thought to me as a sacrifice and I will give them back to you:

Sanctified,

Restored,

Redeemed, and

Set free.

I am with your family and I hear your prayers. I delight in your willingness to move with my Spirit. Well done, my child, well done!

## Mexico Mission Testimony

By Tim Eliasen

My back was injured thirty years ago in a car accident. I've had trouble with it ever since, especially for extended periods of hard manual labor. On the first day of our build in Tecate, I had crippling pain from mixing cement and shoveling sand. By early afternoon, I was kneeling and sitting while mixing, just to help the team accomplish our task.

Nathan laid hands on my back and prayed for healing. Specifically, we prayed that God would release me from the pain that the Enemy brought to try to discourage me. The Evil One attempted to frustrate a plan to bring God's love to Tecate. My back hurt that day, but not on Saturday or Sunday. Usually, the pain would increase with each day, but not this time. The Lord had a mighty plan to be with this community—plans to succeed and not to fail. God is good—all the time!

## Mexico Mission Testimony

By Ken Porter

I had never met Nathan before this Tecate trip. At first, I didn't know what to make of him, but the more time I spent around him—especially after I heard his testimony, the more I realized he was a great man of God. On the second day of our mission trip, my wrist looked like a golf ball was in it. It hurt so badly, I was asking for some pain reliever. Nathan heard me; asked about my pain, and told me I didn't need any pain reliever because we have Jesus and prayer. He grabbed my wrist and asked God to heal every joint, muscle, and tendon. Before that prayer, I was worried that I could not go on, but after that prayer, I went immediately back to work and was able to function in every way. Praise God! Nathan, I have learned a lot from you and saw Jesus in you every day. I thank God that I know you and love you, my friend.

## Back Home at Sunday Church

*Some of the men were asked to give an account of their time while on the Mexico Mission. Many testimonies were shared about changed hearts, but there was not one mention of the many miracles of healing the Lord performed for us.*

# May 18th

**An Unexpected Message**

*A cable guy stopped by the house—a man I did not know. The Lord told me to tell him this:*

I want you to know how much I love you. I heal the broken; I bring the sheep under my shelter. I tell you the truth—I am the Lord your God, maker of heaven and earth. Do not be deceived; my love is endless, my resources are unlimited; get ready for the great adventure.

I am with your mother. Do not be afraid; I make all things new. You are mighty in my sight; you are a part of my royal family. I have heard your prayers, and I brought you to this place tonight to bless you. Know my love—it is endless. I am preparing to unleash my plan in you; just seek me and you will find me and every good thing. I am your provision—I will provide everything you need. I will heal your mind from the damage of drugs; you will be sharp as a tack, and I tell you, nothing shall be impossible for you.

I can tell you that what I am preparing in you is going to be astounding. Spend time with me alone and allow my fullness. Get your pen ready and I will speak in increased measure. I want to save you from yourself. I see you and was there during your darkest hour. I saved you then and I reach out to you now.

I am with your broken family, and I tell you the truth—life is about to get very exciting. Know me and you will know the fullness of my truth. Today is your day, and the rest of your life will be different. You will never be the same. Rest in my truth and remember that I am with you always. Nothing is impossible when you walk close to me.

*Now you understand that I did not know anything about this man. This is another example of how the Lord wants to draw all men to himself, and he will use those who listen to him to help those who do not or to reinforce the validity of what the person may have already been told. The result of this word being given was this: The man burst into tears and asked how I knew these things. I said by the Spirit of the living God. He confirmed that his mother was very ill and that he had used drugs. He said, "It's time I get right with the Lord."*

## My Mighty Movement

I see a map of Washington with a vortex flowing from a heart over Gig Harbor. The heart represents the heart of God which is love. People are being flung from the vortex around the world, and there's a ministry jet flying those who need to minister afar to their destinations. Headlines are being displayed of the stories being written about the phenomenon.

This church—with the revolving pulpit—will rise up to be a voice to the nations. Nothing shall stop my mighty movement:

No gossip—

No lies—

No nonsense—just pure unadulterated motion of mighty power.

This area has never and will never see a more pronounced manifestation of my Spirit. People will fly in from around the globe to be ignited by my Holy Spirit poured out unreservedly, and make no mistake; the harvest will be as a mighty tornado drawing masses to its nucleus.

## Overflow

Get your house in order and I will unleash my seismic phenomenon; gather those as I lead you and reference my instruction. Be willing and I will use what you bring. Give way to my gathering; not one will leave hungry. Everyone who comes will be filled. Overflow is my business, and overflow will pour from your thirsty soul. I have prepared the team and readied each one whom I have called. There will be an outpouring of my holy presence that will bring restoration and repentance on a grand scale, and not one will be able to escape my transformation.

# May 22nd

**Instructions for Building a Church**

I know that you wonder about the

How,

What,

When,

Why, and

Where.

I will reveal every step in detail to the one I have appointed. I will bring more confirmation through each of you so that, collectively, you will not fail. Follow my structure and my instructions as I direct you. I want each of you simply to obey. I'm calling every person to do what I ask, when I ask, and with a good attitude. Submit your selfish ambitions and I will carry you with my heart of love. Do not direct divisions toward those I have appointed—just follow as I lead. I am the Lord your God and I know my plans. Surrender all that you are:

Every thought,

Every ambition,

And I will direct your motion. Give me the right to rule. Then my will will be accomplished, so prepare your hearts to cooperate with my instruction.

# May 23rd

**Leading Leaders**

Direct each one with strong humility and I will lift you up.

> *"Humble yourselves in the sight of the Lord, and He will lift you up."* (James 4:10)

Lead with the encouragement I have given you and remember that I am with you.

> *"Then the messenger who had gone to call Micah spoke to him, saying, "Now listen, the words of the prophets with one accord encourage the king. Please, let your word be like the word of one of them, and speak encouragement."* (1 Kings 22:13)

You do not need to speak any more to be heard, but only speak what I say to speak. Bless those who curse you and give to those who persecute you in my name and your reward will be great.

> *"Bless those who curse you, and pray for those who spitefully use you."* (Luke 6:28)

Follow me and you will be followed. I give detailed instructions so that my work will be done the way I choose.

*"If anyone serves me, let him follow me; and where I am, there my servant will be also. If anyone serves me, him my Father will honor."* (John 12:26)

Love one another and compete not, for I cause you to become great. My words are life to your soul, and I continue to speak here and now. Those of you, who have not completely surrendered to me, do it now.

Everyone desires to be great, and I tell you that you already are—it does not need to be proved; just trust and obey.

> *"Yet it shall not be so among you; but whoever desires to become great among you, let him be your servant."* (Matthew 20:26)

*May 26th*

## The Rock of the Harbor

This church is a result of my Spirit being unleashed on mankind. Guard your hearts; guard your minds; and:

> *"Be anxious for nothing, but in everything by prayer and supplication, with thanksgiving, let your requests be made known to God; and the peace of God, which surpasses all understanding, will guard your hearts and minds through Christ Jesus."* (Philippians 4:6-7)

Work together to exalt one another.

> *"But God is the Judge: He puts down one, and exalts another."* (Psalm 75:7)

My vision is unity—not segregation and competition. Be sure that this mission statement I now give you is published:

Mission Statement: "To present each one mature in the fullness of God, through Jesus Christ our Lord."

## Denominations Unite!

I want to unite spiritually all denominations in love and truth. Denominations are dying. The Rock of the Harbor will be a place that breaks the mold of boxed religion. My love cannot be contained; I want it given outrageously.

People need more—

Churches need more—

Leaders need more—

I have more to give!

If the supernatural has not yet become natural, then hunger needs to be increased; testimony builds faith and increases hunger.

## I Am the Originator

I am the originator.

> *"For by Him all things were created that are in heaven and that are on earth, visible and invisible, whether thrones or dominions or principalities or powers. All things were created through Him and for Him. And He is before all things, and in Him all things consist. And He is the head of the body, the church, who is the beginning, the firstborn from the dead, that in all things He may have the preeminence."* (Colossians 1:16-23)

Who is the terminator?

> *"And they had as king over them the angel of the bottomless pit, whose name in Hebrew is Abaddon, but in Greek he has the name Apollyon."* (Revelation 9:11)

I am the Son of God, and I tell you there is nothing new under me.

> *"That which has been is what will be, that which is done is what will be done, and there is nothing new under the sun."* (Ecclesiastes 1:9)

I am the life so that many will be filled. I am the only way to life everlasting. Know me and you will know the truth.

> *"Jesus said to him, "I am the way, the truth, and the life. No one comes to the Father except through me."* (John 14:6)

Were you your own invention? Of course, what I bring to completion is from the foundations of the earth—not because of any man.

> *"Just as He chose us in Him before the foundation of the world that we should be holy and without blame before Him in love, having predestined us to adoption as sons by Jesus Christ to Himself, according to the good pleasure of His will to the praise of the glory of His grace, by which He made us accepted in the Beloved. In Him we have redemption through His blood, the forgiveness of sins, according to the riches of His grace which He made to abound toward us in all wisdom and prudence having made known to us the mystery of His will, according to His good pleasure which He purposed in Himself that in the dispensation of the fullness of the times He might gather together in one all things in Christ, both which are in heaven and which are on earth—in Him."* (Ephesians 1:4-10)

"Who started the earth?" should be the question—not "Who started the study that motivated another study that motivated the impartation that spurred on the awakening that led to the authorship that opened the eyes to a supernatural gathering that brought on a movement?"

> *"In the beginning God created the heaven and the earth."* (Genesis 1:1)

Everything begins in me and finds its purpose in me so that no man can boast.

*"For by grace you have been saved through faith and that not of yourselves, it is the gift of God, not of works, lest anyone should boast."* (Ephesians 2:8-9)

## Know Me

Know me and you will know my intentions:

To restore,

To redeem,

To sanctify,

To make holy,

To provide,

To prepare,

To produce,

To protect,

To build up,

To resurrect,

To resound,

To reply,

To recommend,

To lead,

To love, and

To liberate.

I want you to guard your lips from saying anything I don't approve.

*"Keep your tongue from evil, and your lips from speaking deceit."*
(Psalm 34:13)

Don't gather support for your opinions; just let slander roll off your back like water off a duck's back.

*"Whoever secretly slanders his neighbor, Him I will destroy; the one who has a haughty look and a proud heart, Him I will not endure."*
(Psalm 101:5)

*"Whoever hides hatred has lying lips, and whoever spreads slander is a fool."* (Proverbs 10:18)

People will say all sorts of things about you; just be sure to maintain purity and I will crush opposition and raise up whom I choose.

*"He who loves purity of heart and has grace on his lips, the king will be his friend."* (Proverbs 22:11)

*"And the God of peace will crush Satan under your feet shortly. The grace of our Lord Jesus Christ be with you. Amen."* (Romans 16:20)

Give me your attention before every decision—big or small.

# May 27th

I know many people have heard the Lord speak to them by his Spirit—a little here and a little there—throughout their lives. This was the case with my mother. As I explored the story of Elijah and Elisha (2 Kings 2), the Lord quickened my Spirit and revealed that he has given us the ability to impart gifts to one another as well as to receive them from the Lord.

"For I long to see you, that I may **impart** to you some spiritual gift, so that you may be established." (Romans 1:11)

"Let no corrupt word proceed out of your mouth, but what is good for necessary edification, that it may **impart** grace to the hearers." (Ephesians 4:2)

Soon after I started hearing the Lord in great measure, I laid hands on my mom and pronounced an impartation to her. I asked that she be given the same ability to hear that I had been given. The following words are one example of how the Lord honored the impartation request. She received these words to give to a struggling single parent.

**The Lord Speaks to a Single Parent**

My daughter, I heard you as you wept before me. I know the agony of your heart. I wish to comfort you, but I also wish to challenge you to follow me to the ends of the earth.

> *"Then he said to them all, "If anyone desires to come after me, let him deny himself, and take up his cross daily, and follow me."* (Luke 9:23)

I have a plan for you, and I will unfold it in the months ahead. I realize you need to work to support yourself and your children, but I will relieve you of that burden. I will bring you someone to help share the load of responsibility you now carry. He is of my choosing, and you will be very pleased for he will fulfill the desires of your heart. He loves me and he will love you and the girls. Please accept him with my blessing.

> *"And the LORD God said, "It is not good that man should be alone; I will make him a helper comparable to him."* (Genesis 2:18)

You have been given a glimpse of what I have planned for this region—a birthing of The Rock of the Harbor where I will pour out my Spirit in great measure. I want you to enter into worship with me there, for you will be strengthened and prepared for future ministry. I don't want you to leave your present fellowship; the Rock will simply be an equipping place where you will be recharged to carry out my will.

I am the Lord your God; I will heal the wounds of your soul.

> *"He heals the brokenhearted and binds up their wounds."* (Psalm 147:3)

*"For I will restore health to you and heal you of your wounds, says the LORD."* (Jeremiah 30:17)

Come to me and drink deep, for the waters I give are a healing balm for your heart, your soul, and your mind.

*"Is there no balm in Gilead, Is there no physician there? Why then is there no recovery for the health of the daughter of my people?"* (Jeremiah 8:22)

I will give you

Singleness of purpose,

Clarity of thought,

Deep satisfaction, and

Peace of mind.

I have many gifts to give which I will lavish on you, my precious daughter.

*"If you then, being evil, know how to give good gifts to your children, how much more will your Father who is in heaven give good things to those who ask him!"* (Matthew 7:11)

June 2011

*June 3rd*

## Sitting in the Driver's Seat

When you sit with me, I surround your innermost thoughts. With great ambition, I move you through to your destiny. I have not reserved anything but have released everything—much more than you have imagined is in process. I have so much to say to you for my purpose of equipping.

> *"And he himself gave some to be apostles, some prophets, some evangelists, and some pastors and teachers, for the equipping of the saints for the work of ministry, for the edifying of the body of Christ, till we all come to the unity of the faith and of the knowledge of the Son of God, to a perfect man, to the measure of the stature of the fullness of Christ."* (Ephesians 4:11-13)

Put your feet in the water and the water will have life poured into it.

> *"After that, he poured water into a basin and began to wash the disciples' feet, and to wipe them with the towel with which he was girded."* (John 13:5)

To be a blessing is an honor and a privilege. Be compelled by compassion and drive forward with force until I bring the full harvest. I do not ever tire of sitting with you.

*I'm sitting on the passenger side of the front seat of a truck talking to the Lord. I heard him say, "Can you see me?" I turned my head to his voice and saw him sitting in the driver's seat, dressed in a white robe. His countenance was beautiful, love flowing from his liquid blue eyes. His wavy, dark brown hair crowned his tanned skin. He placed his hand on my head and said, "Bless you, my child!" Then he disappeared as quickly as he had come.*

All that I am and all that I do is perfecting.

Be my blessing;

Be my gift;

Give yourself away. I want all of you, even your weaknesses.

"And he said to me, "My grace is sufficient for you, for my strength is made perfect in weakness." Therefore most gladly I will rather boast in my infirmities, that the power of Christ may rest upon me." (2 Corinthians 12:9)

Donate my love without expecting to receive and you will be continually filled to overflowing.

# June 6th

**The Rock**

I, Jesus Christ, will pour out to surround those who come to The Rock with living water. Thirst no more for the kingdom of Heaven is at hand.

> *"From that time Jesus began to preach and to say, "Repent, for the kingdom of heaven is at hand." (Matthew 4:17)*

I am the healer; I am the resurrection and the life; no one comes to the Father but by me.

> *"Jesus said to her, "I am the resurrection and the life. he who believes in me, though he may die, he shall live." (John 11:25)*

> *"Jesus said to him, "I am the way, the truth, and the life. No one comes to the Father except through me." (John 14:6)*

Stand on the Rock and know that I made it—the Rock of the Ages.

> *"Therefore whoever hears these sayings of mine, and does them, I will liken him to a wise man who built his house on the rock: and the rain descended, the floods came, and the winds blew and beat*

*on that house; and it did not fall, for it was founded on the rock."*
(Matthew 7:24-25)

If this church were a plan of man, it would surely and quickly fail, but it is the design of heaven. Reflect often on the phrase, "Thy will be done on earth as it is in heaven."

> *"After this manner therefore pray ye: Our Father which art in heaven, hallowed be thy name. Thy kingdom come, thy will be done on earth, as it is in heaven. Give us this day our daily bread and forgive us our debts, as we forgive our debtors. And lead us not into temptation, but deliver us from evil: For thine is the kingdom, and the power, and the glory, for ever. Amen."* (Matthew 6:9-13 KJV)

I will continue to direct you beyond your comfort zone because that is where the growth is.

Some people feel as though they need to decide matters based on their limited understanding, but I say, allow me to be Lord and my will will be naturally revealed and my purposes will be accomplished. Beware of those who stand in the way. I am the Lord God Almighty, maker of heaven and earth, lover of the hurting soul, and I come to bring the abundance of life, and abundance is exactly what you will see.

> *"The thief does not come except to steal, and to kill, and to destroy. I have come that they may have life, and that they may have it more abundantly."* (John 10:10)

Sit with me often;

Learn from me always;

Prepare what I have asked of you and you will not fail.

Victory is the result of battle and the battle rages on.

You have chosen well to be on the winning side of Zion. Blessed are those who hunger for they will be filled.

*"Blessed are those who hunger and thirst for righteousness, for they shall be filled."* (Matthew 5:6)

Now put on your full armor and walk with me.

*"Put on the whole armor of God that you may be able to stand against the wiles of the devil."* (Ephesians 6:11)

Be ready to move by my Spirit; I will direct your path.

*"In all your ways acknowledge him, and he shall direct your paths."* (Proverbs 3:6)

You have what is needed; now press on with a confident conscience and release my message. Anyone who tries to carry a yoke that has not been formed for him will tire and fail.

*"Take my yoke upon you and learn from me, for I am gentle and lowly in heart, and you will find rest for your souls for my yoke is easy and my burden is light."* (Matthew 11:29-30)

No one can carry what has been fashioned for you—I am with you!

# June 7th

## Rhythm and Rhyme

Well springs pour from love's paid debt—
Encountering majestic milestones,
Releasing prolific stiletto.

Destiny's answer to the question unasked;
For the Savior—a simple task.

Tune into my court
And fill me with praise;
For this purpose I made you
To walk in my ways.

When I brushed up against you,
You fell to the floor—
I stood there and watched you
Through the open door.
You knew I was there in spirit and truth
So you came to my side
And I filled you.

Do you wonder why I chose you for this?
Someday I'll share all that's unknown.
For now just listen and tune in to my tone.

I love to give gifts to those who dive in;
I have conquered death and taken all sin.

Every vessel that surrenders to me
Will become my intention
To thrive as a tree,
Bringing life to all who have need,
Conquering self and all forms of greed.

Walk in closeness with hands to the sky,
Hold on loosely and I will provide.
Never changing the ways you should know,
I will show you right where to go.

Peace is surrounding your ankles like sand;
Stand on the Rock and pour out on man.
I will bring forth the waters of life
So all will see my glorious wife.
The veil is torn so I brush it aside,
That her beauty is seen with nothing to hide.

Your heart is my garden and I know what to plant;
Ask for my will and my will I will grant.
Blessings and favor are seeds to be sown;
When weeds are uprooted,
You may hear them groan.

Get what I give you—don't pass it by.
Greatness is willing from El Shaddai.
Package my posture and fly like the wind;
Gracious to all who have been bound by their sin.

I pour in so you can pour out;
Don't try to cork my generous spout.
Give of yourself like a mat under feet,
And you'll be the house I'll make my retreat.

Presence is peace and patience endures;
Healing I bring when it's said there's no cure.
I am the answer to the questions to cure;
To the pain that's been cancelled, my love endures.

No copy can capture,
No generic can bring—
Perfect release of heavenly streams.

# June 8th

## To a Daughter of God

*Why does God choose to single someone out at any given time? I don't know. In this particular situation, the Lord gave me this message for a specific woman—I called her a daughter of God. All I did was write the words down in my journal, which I always carry with me, and then I spoke them to her.*

I delight in your service to me. You are a light of organization. Your willingness to be a blessing to others pleases me. Do not worry for your hurting family—I am with each one. I have gathered them into my loving arms and have felt much compassion for all of them. My will is being made clear as you press into me. Spend more time with me alone in quiet, for there is much I wish to say to you to prepare you for the days ahead. Your life is about to get very exciting. I will reveal my secrets to you and give you the keys to unlock my kingdom so the supernatural becomes natural.

> *"And I will give you the keys of the kingdom of heaven, and whatever you bind on earth will be bound in heaven, and whatever you loose on earth will be loosed in heaven."* (Matthew 16:19)

I see you do to the least of these and I am with you.

*"Then He will answer them, saying, "Assuredly, I say to you, inasmuch as you did not do it to one of the least of these, you did not do it to Me." (Matthew 25:40)*

Your smile reflects my joy in your heart, and you give me glory when you face fear and laugh out loud.

*"He will yet fill your mouth with laughing, and your lips with rejoicing." (Job 8:21)*

Don't be so hard on yourself, for I give grace abounding. Many will try and condemn my chosen children, but I am the Lord your God, maker of heaven and earth. I do not condemn you in any way; you are free and fully accepted in me.

*"There is therefore now no condemnation to those who are in Christ Jesus, who do not walk according to the flesh, but according to the Spirit." (Romans 8:1)*

I love you dearly, and I know my mighty plans that shine brighter every day with the fullness of me—pressed down, stirred up, and overflowing.

*Give and it will be given to you: good measure, pressed down, shaken together, and running over will be put into your bosom. For with the same measure that you use, it will be measured back to you."* (Luke 6:38)

Give unto me your increasing quiet time, for I am the lover of your soul; there is much to do, and I will give you directions in every way. Be bold for the kingdom of Heaven is at hand.

*"Therefore they stayed there a long time, speaking boldly in the Lord, who was bearing witness to the word of his grace, granting signs and wonders to be done by their hands."* (Acts 14:3)

Blessed are you, daughter! I have made you beautiful.

*"He has made everything beautiful in its time. Also he has put eternity in their hearts, except that no one can find out the work that God does from beginning to end."* (Ecclesiastes 3:11)

I see you and I smile with fullness of love. Jump into my arms where the sun has a reason to shine; love unreservedly and you will see my intention.

# June 9th

## Hello, Father

Hello, Son. Be of good cheer for I am with you in every way.

*"These things I have spoken to you, that in me you may have peace. In the world you will have tribulation; but be of good cheer, I have overcome the world."* (John 16:33)

## My Church Will Prosper

I will prosper the Church beyond measure and you will be increasingly glad. Be patient with those who try you, and be gracious to all who accuse you wrongfully.

*"Let the proud be ashamed, for they treated me wrongfully with falsehood; but I will meditate on your precepts."* (Psalm 119:78)

Do not try to win everyone's approval; just move according to my gentle leading and ready yourself for greatness. I am pleased with the way you are leading. People will come from great distances to join my Church body and receive my miracles. Blessed are those who call on my name for I hear and will answer.

## Stand Firm

I turn—

Fears into love,

 Anxiety into peace,

  Confusion into clarity,

   Storms into calm assurance, and

    Wavering into solid direction.

If the winds swirl around you, stand firm in my epicenter heart of love. Raise your hands to me and be my call that consumes all division. Connect my countenance from consequence and rise from the ashes, birthing billows of boldness and beauty. Speak to the storms, although they rage, and they must cease. My words are power on your lips; my holy fire is on your tongue; your jaw is the gate that contains the Lion of the Tribe of Judah, and in me you are its trainer. It roars in the face of fear that sends out confusion and both run for their very lives.

*"I will send my fear before you, I will cause confusion among all the people to whom you come, and will make all your enemies turn their backs to you."* (Exodus 23:27)

## Tornado of Love

I tell you: heaven's fury will be released in you, my faithful, to deliver my tornado of love. Principalities will be shaken from their foundations and strongholds plucked from their pots as young plants.

*"Having disarmed principalities and powers, he made a public spectacle of them, triumphing over them in it."* (Colossians 2:15)

Paradise waits in eager expectation for the **fullness** to be released on the people clinging to defeat.

> *"And He Himself gave some to be apostles, some prophets, some evangelists, and some pastors and teachers, for the equipping of the saints for the work of ministry, for the edifying of the body of Christ, till we all come to the unity of the faith and of the knowledge of the Son of God, to a perfect man, to the measure of the stature of the fullness of Christ; that we should no longer be children, tossed to and fro and carried about with every wind of doctrine, by the trickery of men, in the cunning craftiness of deceitful plotting, but, speaking the truth in love, may grow up in all things into Him who is the head— Christ—from whom the whole body, joined and knit together by what every joint supplies, according to the effective working by which every part does its share, causes growth of the body for the edifying of itself in love."* (Ephesians 4:11-16)

Rise up, my warrior; take back what has been stolen from me—glory robbed from lambs in silence, causing the mighty Rock to cry out and the stones around it, "Give me what is mine and lead others in doing the same."

## Prolific Pandemonium

The earth trembles at the sound of my voice.

I will not be mocked;

   I will not be shaken;

      I will not be ignored.

I will pour out prolific pandemonium and prosper my patient per severer. Make no mistake, I am raising my Church from the grave—it will not avoid my shaking. Fill my storehouse, and as seed, I will multiply my cause. Invite all to share in the harvest of heaven. Open your eyes to all that I am, and consume my goodness, for I cause the blind to see in the Spirit what heaven is holding. Release all that you are on my chosen and submerge yourself in my holy sanctuary. Spring forth with everything you carry and dance on distress with radical transformation.

> *"And the Lord said, "To what then shall I liken the men of this generation and what are they like? They are like children sitting in the marketplace and calling to one another, saying, 'We played the flute for you and you did not dance; we mourned to you and you did not weep.'"* (Luke 7:31-32)

## Contagious Christianity

Your Lord is a consuming fire, burning away the impure and the chaff in need of stripping.

> *"For the LORD your God is a consuming fire, a jealous God."* (Deuteronomy 4:24)

Life is the result of holy fire—raging flames properly placed bring about acceleration of contagious Christianity and duplication of kingdom preparation. Kneel down and ready the council; prepare your heart with peaceful anticipation. This time you will see me move to the full, pressed down and running over—like living streams of living water bringing forth my living Church, causing the dead to live and rise up from routine and religious practices that are rote and disgusting!

> *"He who believes in me, as the scripture has said, out of his heart will flow rivers of living water."* (John 7:38)

I do not wish for my people to work to earn heaven, but rather to enter heaven from a position of rest.

> *"There remains therefore a rest for the people of God. For he who has entered His rest has himself also ceased from his works as God did from His. Let us therefore be diligent to enter that rest, lest anyone fall according to the same example of disobedience."* (Hebrews 4:9-11)

Time with me means more than any task. A great leader gives me time and time captures my heart of love. Recharge your spirit in my presence; renew your strength at my feet.

> *"But those who wait on the LORD shall renew their strength; they shall mount up with wings like eagles, they shall run and not be weary, they shall walk and not faint."* (Isaiah 40:31)

*June 10th*

## Humility Rise Up

Mountains are pushed up from lowly positions—so it is with those who from humility rise up. Exalt me and others before yourself and beware of how you process a compliment.

> *"Let another man praise you, and not your own mouth; a stranger, and not your own lips."* (Proverbs 27:2)

Thank the giver, but know that the gift is from me.

> *"Every good gift and every perfect gift is from above, and comes down from the Father of lights, with whom there is no variation or shadow of turning."* (James 1:17)

Jostling for position, power, influence, or importance springs from:

Rejection,

　　Shame,

　　　　Pride, and

　　　　　　Vanity—

All of which is selfishness. I come to free the captive from the cage of:

Self:

Self-reliance,

Self-centeredness, and

Selfish ambition.

## Mission

"Let me ask you about you so I can tell you about me" is *not* the mission. The mission is to consider everyone more valuable than yourself, but still to lead and bring direction and focus. Someone has to lead as I direct, for this is my way of preventing chaos and promoting peace.

## Significance

When waves crash over your boat, rest in me in quiet and regroup your focus. Everyone has good intentions but will go through stages of temporary blindness. Even the most brilliant minds wander and struggle with the need to feel important and significant. Hide in my love and blanket pride with humble kindness.

> *"Therefore, as the elect of God, holy and beloved, put on tender mercies, kindness, humility, meekness, longsuffering, bearing with one another and forgiving one another, if anyone has a complaint against another; even as Christ forgave you, so you also must do."* (Colossians 3:12-13)

Give attention to my affections because I am your every need.

## Carry My Shield

I love the goals that have been established to carry out my kingdom plan. I say to you, they will be reached. Play the game by my rules and you will win. The ways of man are fading into the night, but my light shines bright on those who submit and step into it. Carry my shield and never stop releasing my words of faith; I use them to breathe on flames for their expansion.

> *"Hold fast the pattern of sound words which you have heard from me, in faith and love which are in Christ Jesus."* (2 Timothy 1:13)

I view jostling for position juvenile, and I wish for each to be made mature in me, finding that one's real life is found in losing it. Die to self and be that which is trampled and offense will roll off your back.

## Earthly Wisdom

Penetratus (Latin for penetrate), research and study are good, but no earthly wisdom can trump the life words of heaven, for I know the end from the beginning and the beginning from the end.

> *"But if you have bitter envy and self-seeking in your hearts, do not boast and lie against the truth. This wisdom does not descend from above, but is earthly, sensual, and demonic. For where envy and self-seeking exist, confusion and every evil thing are there."* (James 3:14-16)

Whose knowledge is greater than its inventor? **Is man his own creation birthed of science or is science birthed from man's intent to wrap futility around creation's divinity?** I have made man in my image, but truly, man is limited and lifeless without my very breath.

*"Then God said, "Let us make man in our image, according to our likeness; let them have dominion over the fish of the sea, over the birds of the air, and over the cattle, over all the earth and over every creeping thing that creeps on the earth." (Genesis 1:26)*

## Supernatural vs. Natural

Free yourself of the graphs, percentages, and trends of statistics. Rid yourselves of studying research data and odds. The supernatural cannot be fully explained in the natural; only the wisdom of heaven can make sense of heaven's kingdom.

## Born of Hunger

I love those who ask for wisdom, born of hunger, to help others to freedom. I will enjoy reconciling the reckless and preparing the patient. Be certain of my directives, and then proceed with boldness in the direction of my Spirit. My word is alive, even now.

*"For the word of God is living and powerful, and sharper than any two-edged sword, piercing even to the division of soul and spirit, and of joints and marrow, and is a discerner of the thoughts and intents of the heart." (Hebrews 4:12)*

## A Mighty Stir

Many are the times I have wanted to gather my chicks, but they would not be gathered.

*"O Jerusalem, Jerusalem, the one who kills the prophets and stones those who are sent to her! How often I wanted to gather your children together, as a hen gathers her chicks under her wings, but you were not willing!" (Matthew 23:37)*

Now I will cause a mighty stir and my people will flock to me in great numbers, for they will know that I am God, and they will come to me for protection from the great evil that would seek to devour them. I said I will shake my Church, and I surely will; I will shake them so that they will be sifted—the chaff from the wheat; the real from fake—those who only have a form of godliness but deny my power.

*"His winnowing fan is in his hand, and he will thoroughly clean out his threshing floor, and gather his wheat into the barn; but he will burn up the chaff with unquenchable fire."* (Matthew 3:12)

*"But know this, that in the last days perilous times will come: For men will be lovers of themselves, lovers of money, boasters, proud, blasphemers, disobedient to parents, unthankful, unholy, unloving, unforgiving, slanderers, without self-control, brutal, despisers of good, traitors, headstrong, haughty, lovers of pleasure rather than lovers of God, having a form of godliness but denying its power. And from such people turn away!"* (2 Timothy 3:1-5)

## Politics in Washington

I have restrained my hand of judgment on this country long enough. I am tired of the lies coming out of Washington D.C. so I will start my fire in Washington State and it will be felt beyond all *borders*! I will raise up politicians who have my Spirit within them and who are willing to expose themselves to the pack of wolves in Washington. These political warriors will be given power to endure the onslaughts they will encounter and will work in tandem with my efforts to renew my Church. My efforts will produce the desired result for I never work in vain—some will say I'm a mover and a shaker!

# June 11th

## We Do Not Have Forty Years!

*The Lord directed these words to the leaders of The Rock of the Harbor equipping center, but they would be appropriate for any group of leaders trying to work together to achieve a common goal. In this case, it was to start a church.*

You are in place for my purpose and not your own. I am the Lord your God, maker of heaven and earth. I know my plans—do you not know my voice? I have called each one of you, but not because of your own qualifications. I am preparing to use your strengths and your weaknesses for my purposes. Will you follow my structure? I sent Moses to lead through desert lands to what was promised. I want the Rock to be struck the way I direct—we do not have forty years!

> *"Behold, I will stand before you there on the rock in Horeb; and you shall strike the rock, and water will come out of it that the people may drink." And Moses did so in the sight of the elders of Israel."* (Exodus 17:6)

My plan must proceed now. Support one another and remember that I am with you. I have asked one to step out of the boat first; follow his lead and my kingdom will be duplicated. Get your eyes on me and I will calm your internal storm. I will move you into exactly what you were made to do:

Some to teach;

Some to evangelize;

Some to prophesy;

Some to worship;

Some to intercede;

Some to do some part of these, and

Some to do all of these.

True surrender is not offended. Spend time with me alone; expose the darkness in your own hearts. I will use each of you for my mighty call.

## Division among Men

The Enemy is lurking—trying to find a way to get a foothold that leads to a stronghold, in order to cause division. Do not allow yourself to be his puppet; rather stand firm against him and worship me and he will flee.

> *"Therefore submit to God. Resist the devil and he will flee from you."*
> (James 4:7)

Everything that has been established has come to pass in sequence. Will you bring me your burdens? Will you surrender all? You know I have called each of you to greatness—do not let pride minimize the magnitude of my plan. In me, you have everything. You have been gathered for something much bigger than yourself.

# June 12th

## Gatekeeper

My Spirit cannot be packaged nor can it be contained.

Love will draw those who lack it;

Peace will surround those who are centered by it;

Focus will fill my appointed; and

Grace will cover my anointed.

I will carry my baby and protect him from harm. Patient, prosperous, planner—prepare a pinnacle penthouse. I am the gatekeeper of your mouth; when you surrender it to me, I will direct what is spoken and shut it to avoid wrong talk.

*"A word fitly spoken is like apples of gold in settings of silver."* (Proverbs 25:11)

## Masterpiece of My Intention

Lay it all down.

*"No one takes it from me, but I lay it down of myself. I have power to lay it down, and I have power to take it again. This command I have received from my Father."* (John 10:18)

I will:

Restore, and

   Replace, and

      Increase, and

         Hold on, and

            Release.

Come through my open door and walk to me that you will be filled with heaven. Allow my presence to lift you into pages of love not yet read—not yet captured. Pour out my life to the thirsty and gardens will rise up from the dying seeds, broken for me. Place your substance into my hands that I can mold you into the masterpiece of my intention, resting to renew you back into loving service.

## Wisdom Dances

Life's wisdom dances on the corners of priceless moments spent soaking in my goodness. See my stages blossom like the springtime flower planted by streams of solace. Melodies surround the presence of holiness and open arms wait for the desperately discouraged heart in need of filling.

## Confusion Will Flee

Be the reason I shine;

Be the joy set before me;

Become the balance between heaven's hand and hell's fury;

Reach out and cling to my fingers, stretched down to lift you from desperation;

Balance on my clarity,

Lean on my understanding, and

I will cause confusion to flee the torment of all that is righteous.

Every weapon formed against what I have protected will be pointed back to the assailer—justice jumping from sailing shores, crashing upon what is solid.

*"No weapon formed against you shall prosper, and every tongue which rises against you in judgment you shall condemn. This is the heritage of the servants of the LORD, and their righteousness is from me," says the LORD."* (Isaiah 54:17)

# June 13th

## A Struggling Leader

Balance is important and my word is perfect balance. When you fail, start again; when you fall short, stand up.

> *"Do not rejoice over me, my enemy; when I fall, I will arise; when I sit in darkness, The LORD will be a light to me."* (Micah 7:8)

I have you on a path of accelerated leadership. You are running past the obstacles of the Enemy and the remnants are Basic Principles of Biblical Studies.

Stand tall;

Stand firm;

Bless those who wish to discredit you for they know not what I have made you.

You are my mighty servant;

You are my stronghold strainer;

You string up Satan's sabotage and send him seething.

Darkness hides from your entrance; and

My armor surrounds you like the plates of a tank.

*"Therefore take up the whole armor of God that you may be able to withstand in the evil day, and having done all, to stand."* (Ephesians 6:13)

## A Name

*What do we call ourselves, Lord?*

You are The Rock of the Harbor, a church for churches, embracing all with the love of God as an equipping center with fullness.

## To a Jewish Leader

*A prophetic word given to my mom, Betty French...*

You are one of my chosen ones; one whose eyes have been opened to the fact that I am the great I am. My people have been blinded—they didn't know me when I came, but you—nearly two thousand years later—know who I am. Bless you, my mighty humble servant. I will build you and your little flock into a mighty standing oak. Many will find shelter and protection under your branches.

My benediction is upon you, and I have sealed that benediction with mighty angels who will guard you and protect you, blessing all who enter your doors. Even now, they are stationed above the square building you meet in. How fitting that you call yourselves a four-square church, meeting in a four-square building, blessed by my angels who come from a city four-square.

*"And he who talked with me had a gold reed to measure the city, its gates, and its wall. The city is laid out as a square; its length is as great as its breadth. And he measured the city with the reed: twelve thousand furlongs. Its length, breadth, and height are equal. Then he measured its wall: one hundred and forty-four cubits, according to the measure of a man, that is, of an angel."* (Revelation 21:15-17)

Rise up, my mighty warrior, and continue to march to the call of the shofar.

Come to me often for guidance; Look to me and I will guide you with my eye.

*"I will instruct you and teach you in the way you should go; I will guide you with my eye."* (Psalm 32:8)

You will help usher in my kingdom. I have specific work for you to do, and I will make it known to you in steps. You have been laboring in my fields; now I want you to rest in me until I give you the word to go. I will draw all men to me and you will help to nurture my sheep.

Let joy overflow;

Let words of encouragement flow from your mouth to your flock;

Let my healing waters run freely; and

Let my words bring sustenance to your soul.

Do not allow discouragement to gain a foothold—you have nothing to be discouraged about. Don't judge your effectiveness by the size of your flock; judge your effectiveness by how readily you love and obey me. I am pleased with you, my son—I am greatly pleased. Let's move together now for the task set before us; follow closely because I am going to upset my Church at large, and the way I do things are not the way they have been done. Come! This is a new adventure, and you will need to follow me closely. Halleluiah!

# June 18th

## A Word to Our Family

*This is another word given to my mother but directed this time to our entire family. The wisdom contained here can apply to any family, but I include it to show how deeply God cares for the family as a unit and how powerful the influence of a family can be when committed to him.*

Don't try to clean yourself up before you come to me—come to me first and I will wash you with my waters of forgiveness. I am the kingdom and the power and the glory forever, and I place my kingdom and power in the hearts of my followers for my glory.

*"And do not lead us into temptation, but deliver us from the evil one. For yours is the kingdom and the power and the glory forever. Amen." (Matthew 6:13)*

I will give rest to your souls; there is no need to strive. Then I will help you rebuild your lives, one step at a time. Covering sin only causes internal pain; exposing it to my light begins the process of conquering it.

*"This is the message which we have heard from him and declare to you, that God is light and in him is no darkness at all." (1 John 1:5)*

Sin happens when you act on the promptings of the evil one—when you agree with him. Victory happens when you agree with me and act on that belief.

I do not leave you alone to work out the details of your life; I give you assistance through my Bible words, through the Holy Spirit within you, and through the fellowship of my saints. I want to speak to you. I want you to move from your self-centered concerns to other-centered concerns. There is a lost and dying world out there, and I do not wish for any to perish.

> *"The Lord is not slack concerning his promise, as some count slackness, but is longsuffering toward us, not willing that any should perish but that all should come to repentance."* (2 Peter 3:9)

I want you to move beyond yourselves so you can help with my harvest. I want you to be spiritual farmers.

> *"Do you not say, 'There are still four months and then comes the harvest'? Behold, I say to you, lift up your eyes and look at the fields, for they are already white for harvest!"* (John 4:35)

Believe me when I say, it will be the most rewarding experience of your lives. Pray for one another and support one another.

> *"Confess your trespasses to one another, and pray for one another, that you may be healed. The effective, fervent prayer of a righteous man avails much."* (James 5:16)

Use what money you have wisely and I will give you an increase. The increase will be based on your obedience. If you sow to destruction, you will reap destruction. Give me what is mine and I will return it to you many times.

It will be fun for you to go through the rebuilding of your lives with me. Yes, there will be areas that need to be torn down before they can be built up again; however, the end result will be magnificent. Don't delay; come to me now. I want to get started for the time is short before I come for my bride, the Church. **Remember that delayed obedience is disobedience.**

*June 19th*

## A Precious Moment

Here you are again sitting with me in obedience to my prompting. There are so many adjustments and corrections and revelations I am carrying you through. Right now is a precious moment as I convey my next message to you. I consider all things in my instructions.

Peace is my posture;

    Restoration is my reason;

        Constant is my cleansing; and

            Calculated is my cause.

## Intercessors

Do you know what I'm preparing? Do you know the scale or the magnitude? The grand nature of what I am releasing is going to need to be soaked in prayer. Assemble your team of intercessors.

*"Pray without ceasing."* (1 Thessalonians 5:17)

Release my clarity. Don't be concerned with what is not happening—be focused on what is. Focus on me constantly and pray until my peace upon you is full. You will not need to be defending yourself; just find out what is needed from me; then simply apply love, acceptance, restoration, and life—these are all needed. If rejection is apparent, pour out my love and I will replenish your supply. When you grow weary, rest in me and I will lift you up.

> *"And let us not grow weary while doing good, for in due season we shall reap if we do not lose heart."* (Galatians 6:9)

Fight the good fight of faith and I will be your secret weapon.

> *"Fight the good fight of faith, lay hold on eternal life, to which you were also called and have confessed the good confession in the presence of many witnesses."* (1 Timothy 6:12)

## Adversity

In the midst of adversity, my life springs forth from the rock.

> *"If you faint in the day of adversity, your strength is small."* (Proverbs 24:10)

In the absence of fear is the home of perfect love.

> *"There is no fear in love; but perfect love casts out fear, because fear involves torment. But he who fears has not been made perfect in love."* (1 John 4:18)

In the presence of peace is the abundance of joy.

The longing for righteousness brings coveted beginnings.

Hunger is the activator to holiness and purity.

Giving ourselves away brings emptiness to filling, running over that which is lowly. Curiosity and diligence brings heaven's answer.

Humility is the wellspring of life.

Remain in my presence and you will open many gifts.

Unlock closed doors with laughter from faith, and they will be opened.

Settle your mind in me and rest in everything I say and do.

## I Am Love

Everything I am is from love because I am love.

*"We love him because he first loved us."* (1 John 4:19)

When you sit with me:

- I surround you and refresh you like taking a shower for the first time in many days.

- I forgive what has made you unclean and call you to cleanliness.

- I redeem.

- I sanctify.

- I give good gifts to those who deny themselves.

- I pour into those who empty out all that is born of my spirit, recharging their fruit of kindness, replenishing their stock of grace and mercy, and supplying all that is lacking.

# June 20th

## Supernatural Caffeine

You enjoy coffee—the taste, the smell, the warmth. In the same way, I love to enjoy you enjoying my presence and peace. Giving me your time is like supernatural caffeine—I energize your Spirit and you become boosted in your ability to perform without side effects.

Be encouraged this day that great things are happening all around you. I long for you to be constantly filled with my Spirit so you can dance on distress and leap over what has drawn you from me.

> *"And do not be drunk with wine, in which is dissipation; but be filled with the Spirit, speaking to one another in psalms and hymns and spiritual songs, singing and making melody in your heart to the Lord."* (Ephesians 5:18-19)

Your attention is my reward; your growing understanding is a delight to my nostrils—like a beautiful perfume. I will appear to you again today to confirm that I am moving with you to accomplish my purpose. When I call you—come; when temptation comes—run.

> *"No temptation has overtaken you except such as is common to man; but God is faithful, who will not allow you to be tempted beyond*

*what you are able, but with the temptation will also make the way of escape, that you may be able to bear it."* (1 Corinthians 10:13)

I am delighting in your interaction. Yes, you saw me sit down. Be still in my presence and know that I am—that I am—that I am!

# June 21st

## I Commission You

Paradise proclaims the wonders of the kingdom of the Living God! I release you fully to fulfill your destiny. I send you now commissioned for greatness to wake my sleeping Church Bride. Remember that every moment I go with you in power and might to tear down strongholds and to fill those who hunger and thirst.

> *"For though we walk in the flesh, we do not war according to the flesh, for the weapons of our warfare are not carnal but mighty in God for pulling down strongholds, casting down arguments and every high thing that exalts itself against the knowledge of God, bringing every thought into captivity to the obedience of Christ."* (2 Corinthians 10:3-5)

Give away my kingdom and my kingdom will be released in, upon, and around those who will turn their ears—those who will tune to the tone of my voice, the frequency of heaven unleashed on mankind to carry out the purposes of God the Father. Restore my fractured flock—

Separated,

  Isolated, and

    Broken.

Be my hands; be my feet; run to greet my hosts into the victory that has been won. Fight from victory and you will not be rocked from that which is solid.

# June 22nd

**I Surrender**

*The Lord has asked me to start a church and I am in a state of confusion. "Am I really called?" I say to him, "I surrender to your will, Lord."*

**I Have Called You**

Do not accept a mindset of confusion.

> *"For God is not the author of confusion but of peace, as in all the churches of the saints."* (1 Corinthians 14:33)

Just rest now; relax and cast your cares on me.

> *"Therefore humble yourselves under the mighty hand of God, that he may exalt you in due time, casting all your care upon him, for he cares for you."* (1 Peter 5:6-7)

I want you to start this Church. It is my will that you move in my Spirit. I have called you to lead this movement by my direction, and I will lead through you. There is a time to lead and a time to be led. It is not easy to lead leaders, and it is impossible without my voice. To say that no prophetic words are going to be needed for direction would be an ignorant statement. I will not mention that I have called you to start this magnificent manifestation of majesty again. Stop clamoring, and again, only say what I tell you to say, and do what I ask of you. Keep your walk pure; give no access to the thief to come in and steal.

A great leader will submit to me;

A great leader is humble;

A great leader is dependable;

A great leader is calculated;

A great leader is responsible;

A great leader listens,

A great leader trusts in me;

A great leader obeys my orders, and

A great leader is hungry.

## A Pastor in Training

You will start as the pastor of The Rock of the Harbor. I will draw those I call to join you in my movement. You are a pastor in training. I have given you the plans and the specific blueprint will be revealed in stages. I want you to lead with my words: Test them—yes. Deny them—no!

# June 24th

## Do Not Be Discouraged

Read Matthew and I will reveal my secrets. Do not be discouraged; I cause all things to work together for good.

> *"For consider him who endured such hostility from sinners against himself, lest you become weary and discouraged in your souls."* (Hebrews 12:3)

> *"And we know that all things work together for good to those who love God, to those who are called according to his purpose."* (Romans 8:28)

Those who attack you—born from jealousy or strife, will answer to me, your defender. I have called you to lead these men as I myself led. How could this not be biblical when I am perfect theology? Will you allow me to turn the ears of the hearer toward me? I will expose all forms of evil myself in my time. Let the lies fall on deaf ears and all that I have prepared will prosper. I forgive all who challenge my directives, but beware to anyone who blasphemes my Holy Spirit.

I am the one who appoints;

  I am the one who anoints;

    I am the one who calls out order.

Each will lead when I speak the order, and the order must be obeyed. Do not allow yourself to be bullied into a corner. Rise up and press into opposition and I will go before you!

> *"The* LORD *your God, who goes before you, he will fight for you, according to all he did for you in Egypt before your eyes, and in the wilderness where you saw how the* LORD *your God carried you, as a man carries his son, in all the way that you went until you came to this place."* (Deuteronomy 1:29-31)

# June 25th

**A Reprimand to Church Leaders**

I, the Lord your God, speak to you, men of The Rock of the Harbor.

It is I who will use your weakness,

It is I who appoint, and

It is I who anoint.

Do you dare test the authority of heaven? Bow down your pride and willfulness and do not be deceived. Bind the spirits of:

Witchcraft Control,

Sabotage,

Fear, and

False Accusation.

*"And I will give you the keys of the kingdom of heaven, and whatever you bind on earth will be bound in heaven, and whatever you loose on earth will be loosed in heaven."* (Matthew 16:19)

Work to seek me through prayer and fasting for my order.

*"So Jesus said to them, "Because of your unbelief; for assuredly, I say to you, if you have faith as a mustard seed, you will say to this mountain, 'Move from here to there,' and it will move; and nothing will be impossible for you. However, this kind does not go out except by prayer and fasting."* (Matthew 17:20-22)

Do not let my structure cause any to feel rejection. Search your own hearts. Lay down your selfishness; surrender yourselves one to another and submit yourselves to my direction. Where were you when I created the earth?

*"Where were you when I laid the foundations of the earth? Tell me, if you have understanding."* (Job 38:4)

Do you not know that it was my hand that called you to order? Why do you seek to discredit the one whom I have appointed? Do not judge as the Devil and condemn as the wicked. Rise up from your arrogance and realize it is not you who are the Rock—it is I.

*"The LORD lives! Blessed be my Rock! Let God be exalted, The Rock of my salvation!"* (2 Samuel 22:47)

How much of a reminder will you need? Lay yourself down in surrender and do as I have called you—UNIFY! Let the greatest of all be the servant to all.

*"And he sat down, called the twelve, and said to them, "If anyone desires to be first, he shall be last of all and servant of all."* (Mark 9:35)

# June 27th

## I Am Your Defender

Why do you worry about defending yourself? I am your defender. Do not worry how to proceed; just declare that you will not allow the world to squeeze you into its own mold, but that you will make decisions based on what I say.

> *"Don't let the world around you squeeze you into its own mold, but let God re-mold your minds from within, so that you may prove in practice that the plan of God for you is good, meets all his demands and moves toward the goal of true maturity."* (Romans 12:1)[1]

Do not seek to obey man's agenda. You will submit yourself to each whom I have appointed; however, your first commitment is to obey me, your Lord, above all else. Wisdom is found in a multitude of counselors, and you will seek wisdom and consider counsel from every man on the team.

> *"Where there is no counsel, the people fall; but in the multitude of counselors there is safety."* (Proverbs 11:14)

1 (J.B. Phillips New Testament)

Their voice *does* matter, but my voice is what you are to obey.

## God's Way of Dealing with Division in the Church

I ask you leaders of The Rock of the Harbor *not* to participate in discussions that cause dissension or division within our fold. If you have a problem with your brother, go to him in private in love. If he does not receive you, then bring two with you; if he still does not receive you, bring him before our team.

> *"Moreover if your brother sins against you, go and tell him his fault between you and him alone. If he hears you, you have gained your brother. But if he will not hear, take with you one or two more, that 'by the mouth of two or three witnesses every word may be established."* (Matthew 18:14-16)

Under no circumstances will spiritual wickedness divide with "anger disguised as love." This is a team—the Lord is the owner and author. I have been appointed coach and the twelve are the players on the team. Our task is to serve God by serving others. Again, we are an equipping center on the fullness of God, appointed and anointed to serve Him by serving others.

Peace and harmony are achieved in surrender. When we give ourselves away and expect nothing in return, we are given much more than we ever imagined. Let us change the way we do church and let the Holy Spirit have his way. Equipping Center, Fullness of God, Non-competing! If we are non-competing and we are here to serve, then we are no longer a secret and do not threaten our standing nor commitments with our current churches. The Rock, which is Jesus, will begin next Sunday, July 10, 2011, 2:00 p.m. Bless the Lord, oh my soul—may all that is within us bless his holy name.

*"Bless the LORD, O my soul; and all that is within me, bless his holy name! Bless the Lord, O my soul, and forget not all his benefits: who forgives all your iniquities, who heals all your diseases."* (Psalm 103:1-3)

# June 30th

**An Example of Myself**

*As my mother was praying for me, the Lord gave her these words to help her understand what God is doing in me.*

I want to use Nathan as an example of myself; therefore, I want him to experience what I have also experienced. He will learn to stand alone, to be dependent on me for affirmation instead of looking to man to meet that need. You will always have friends if you are operating according to their desires, but when you cannot meet their expectations, they will quickly tire of you. If you pander to their pride, they will stroke you in return, but if you expose their pride, they will soon shun you. There is a friend who sticks closer than a brother—that is me.

> *"A man who has friends must himself be friendly, but there is a friend who sticks closer than a brother."* (Proverbs 18:24)

I will never leave you nor forsake you; your heart can fully trust and rely on me and my goodness.

> *"And the LORD, He is the One who goes before you. He will be with you; He will not leave you nor forsake you; do not fear nor be dismayed."* (Deuteronomy 31:8)

You may feel alone, but you are not really alone—I am with you and I will continue to bless you as my Father blesses me.

## Twelve Pillars

The twelve pillars will be reestablished and they will truly be tight. They will support one another and my words, newly given, will be confirmed and revered. Doubt and unbelief will be things of the past—trust and obedience will reign. Mighty exploits will be done in my name and my servants will not scramble to take the credit; they will defer to one another in meekness and lowliness of heart. Blame will be replaced by flame! Dross will be consumed, leaving pure gold reflecting my glory. My Church will be purified and many looking on will eagerly want to join the ranks of my beloved.

## A Conquering Army

The Enemy will become sorely vexed and will leave before the intensity of my holy presence. Sin will be openly revealed and forgiven, preparing the way for victory. My Church will go forward boldly, as a mighty conquering army, and nothing will stand in its way. My words, both written and spoken, will give strength to the right hand of my salvation, and I will reign supreme in the hearts of those who are willing. Selah *(think about that)*.

July 2011

# July 3rd

**Free Will**

Remember that free will does affect my best plan.

*"And when you offer a sacrifice of thanksgiving to the LORD, offer it of your own free will."* (Leviticus 22:29)

There are words I give you that are my best plan and when my best is not sought, my best is not received, and therefore, it would seem my word is not accurate. Now if I say it could happen, it is a suggestion, but it does not have to be because I have many ways of accomplishing my purpose. The easiest way to get to my best is total surrender. There is a way that seems right to a man—a way of figuring things out that is very intellectual and lacks heavenly wisdom and godly direction.

*"There is a way that seems right to a man, but its end is the way of death."* (Proverbs 14:12)

# July 4th

## Your Servant is Listening, Lord

When you come to me expecting to hear, I activate my Spirit inside of you. Prepare yourself for my fullness by taking time like this for me to speak to you.

> *"So he gave them his attention, expecting to receive something from them."* (Acts 3:5)

I have reserved the name, The Rock of the Harbor, and no one can take it from you. Those who are not willing to follow my structure will fall back, and I will raise up those who will obey me. Don't give a lot of attention to false accusation; just keep my life in you complete. I have called you to serve and obey. Believe in my perfect plan.

> *"Now the Spirit expressly says that in latter times some will depart from the faith, giving heed to deceiving spirits and doctrines of demons, speaking lies in hypocrisy, having their own conscience seared with a hot iron, forbidding to marry, and commanding to abstain from foods which God created to be received with thanksgiving by those who believe and know the truth. For every creature of God is good, and nothing is to be refused if it is received with thanksgiving;*

*for it is sanctified by the word of God and prayer. If you instruct the brethren in these things, you will be a good minister of Jesus Christ, nourished in the words of faith and of the good doctrine which you have carefully followed. But reject profane and old wives' fables, and exercise yourself toward godliness. For bodily exercise profits a little, but godliness is profitable for all things, having promise of the life that now is and of that which is to come. This is a faithful saying and worthy of all acceptance. For to this end we both labor and suffer reproach, because we trust in the living God, who is the Savior of all men, especially of those who believe. These things command and teach. Let no one despise your youth, but be an example to the believers in word, in conduct, in love, in spirit, in faith, in purity. Till I come, give attention to reading, to exhortation, to doctrine. Do not neglect the gift that is in you, which was given to you by prophecy with the laying on of the hands of the eldership. Meditate on these things; give yourself entirely to them, that your progress may be evident to all. Take heed to yourself and to the doctrine. Continue in them, for in doing this you will save both yourself and those who hear you."* (1 Timothy 4)

# July 6th

## Is It Possible?

Why not now?

Why not you?

Why not abundant?

Ask yourself whether it is possible to have what you dream. I tell you that nothing is impossible.

*"For with God nothing will be impossible."* (Luke 1:37)

I did not call you to poverty; I called you to abundance and prosperity. Keep your perspective and listen to my voice carefully. I will give you the desires of your heart; just do what I have asked of you and rely on my direction.

## Twelve Men

I have chosen twelve men, according to their gifts, not to stay in one place but to make disciples of me—to rotate in and then rotate out—and to remain as pillars in my house of holiness. The leadership will not be limited to twelve, but it will begin with those I have chosen. Welcome to my equipping center! Come and experience my fullness, pressed down and spilling over. Be my blessing!

*July 9th*

## The Rock of the Harbor Beginning

*Another prophetic word given to my mother for The Rock…*

I will pour out on this small gathering who expect great things from me,

> Who trust in small beginnings, and

> > Who are obedient to me.

This gathering is not about one leader or many—it is about my grace poured out on mankind, preparing them for my coming and for the end of the age.

> *"Go therefore and make disciples of all the nations, baptizing them in the name of the Father and of the Son and of the Holy Spirit, teaching them to observe all things that I have commanded you; and lo, I am with you always, even to the end of the age." Amen.*
> (Matthew 28:19-20)

As you've been reading about the needy people who came to me when I walked the dusty streets of Galilee, so the same kinds of needs will be represented by those who gather at the harbor. And, just as I healed the sick and cast out demons long ago, I will, by the power of my Holy Spirit, do the same through my servant Nathan and the twelve pillars that will be faithful. My power will not be limited to these few men, but it will be made manifest through them in great measure so that all will know I am moving in a way not seen in this generation.

*July 11th*

## First Gathering of The Rock

Well done, faithful servant!

> *"His lord said to him, 'Well done, good and faithful servant; you were faithful over a few things, I will make you ruler over many things. Enter into the joy of your lord."* (Matthew 25:21)

You have obeyed me above all odds and the kickoff was successful—a great beginning to start my mighty movement. Do not be overwhelmed; just take one step at a time and know that I am with you—no mountain is too high.

*July 16th*

## A Love Poem from God

What will I to do? What will I to say?
Where will I send thee? What will thou pray?

All that I am making is of heaven's accord;
I can say you'll never be bored.

Get what you can from my masterful gifts;
You asked and I've answered with more than your list.

Preparing my pouring for passions afford;
What I will give you will rock your gourd.

You thought you had seen my blessings abound,
But only the surface has touched this still town.

Gather my goodness, new life I will bring;
Surely you'll notice by the songs that you sing.

Let go of all worry and rest in my love;
Release my good measure as light as the dove.

Peaceful as pastures teeming with life;
I have given you a beautiful wife.

Cherish her goodness while she's by your side
And show all who see you what not to divide.

For what I put together is meant to be good;
Many will see and do as they should.

I came to show the greatest is love,
Pressed down and poured out from heaven above.

I smile when I see you reading my word;
Your hunger rewarded. My spirit you've heard.

Pleasantly speaking to the deep of your soul;
Healed and revived is always my goal.

Try on what's been trampled and glean my rare pearls;
So you too can share my hope with your girls.

The most precious of memories for me are new births;
You can only imagine how much is your worth.

Time will tell, as it has told
How much life can change when you learn to be bold.

No one can keep you from walking in light,
Nor can he steal your air born delight.

I'm holding your hand so you cannot fall;
Hold back your shoulders and stand up tall.

I've given my words to lead others to life;
Now splash them all over and fight the good fight!

**Church Done God's Way**

Stop and listen to the sound of my voice.

Leave behind continually your own ambitions.

Give me your whole heart so I can direct it.

I am preparing a layer of love to be released upon all who come.

Don't worry about anything—I have cared for every part of my cause.

Give time to sharing my word in Matthew and enjoy worship.

It does not need to be perfect—just true.

Freely move with me and I will freely move through you.

Acknowledge all who come and enjoy their uniqueness.

Bask in my blessings.

Give me your focus and I will direct what you see.

Place your awareness in my sanctuary and fill me with praise that tears down strongholds.

*"For though we walk in the flesh, we do not war according to the flesh for the weapons of our warfare are not carnal but mighty in God for pulling down strongholds, casting down arguments and every high thing that exalts itself against the knowledge of God, bringing every thought into captivity to the obedience of Christ."* (2 Corinthians 10:3-5)

Give me all you are and I will fill you with all I am.

Real life is found in losing it.

*"He who finds his life will lose it, and he who loses his life for my sake will find it."* (Matthew 10:39)

I want surrender. I want obedience.

*"Behold, to obey is better than sacrifice."* (1 Samuel 15:22)

*July 18th*

## Dream of Seduction

You were temped in your dreams and your wife was also tempted last night. The power of seduction is subtle and strong—this will need to be carefully handled and quickly and harshly avoided. The Enemy has set traps for you and your wife to be tested and I will allow these tests. If you pass them, you will receive your reward—if you fail, it will make your life difficult. So be on guard for the power of Witchcraft Seduction and Medusa and be sure to bind and loose.

> *"And I will give you the keys of the kingdom of heaven, and whatever you bind on earth will be bound in heaven, and whatever you loose on earth will be loosed in heaven."* (Matthew 16:19)

I am capable of destroying every stronghold.

> *"For the weapons of our warfare are not carnal but mighty in God for pulling down strongholds, casting down arguments and every high thing that exalts itself against the knowledge of God, bringing every thought into captivity to the obedience of Christ."* (2 Corinthians 10:4-5)

Resist the Devil and he will flee from you.

*"Therefore, submit to God. Resist the devil and he will flee from you."* (James 4:7)

## Ready Your Escape

Do not let your guard down, but be on guard and ready your escape. The Destroyer is lurking because of the magnitude of the ministry call on your union. You and your wife have joined together, and both will experience a very strong anointing. I am increasing it as you pass the test of your mind where your thoughts live.

> *"For this is the covenant that I will make with the house of Israel after those days, says the LORD: I will put my laws in their mind and write them on their hearts; and I will be their God, and they shall be My people."* (Hebrews 8:10)

Sin is born first in the thoughts; then once conceived gives way to all forms of destruction.

> *"But Jesus, knowing their thoughts, said, "Why do you think evil in your hearts?"* (Matthew 9:4)

> *"Let this mind be in you which was also in Christ Jesus, who, being in the form of God, did not consider it robbery to be equal with God, but made Himself of no reputation, taking the form of a bondservant, and coming in the likeness of men."* (Philippians 2:5-7)

## Battle Ready

My favor is upon you;

My life is within you;

My armor is full, and

You are ready for battle!

*"Put on the whole armor of God that you may be able to stand against the wiles of the devil."* (Ephesians 6:11)

Give me your attentions and I will give you my wisdom and protection from any enemy who tries to sneak into your camp while you are sleeping. All I am and all I do is from love. Watch for the counterfeit—the one who leads to ruined lives and lonely despair—and continue your efforts. Blessed are the poor in spirit for theirs is the kingdom of Heaven. Blessed are you, my peacemaker!

*"Blessed are the poor in spirit, for theirs is the kingdom of heaven."* (Matthew 5:3)

*"Blessed are the peacemakers, for they shall be called sons of God."* (Matthew 5:9)

## July 19th

**I Come as a River**

When I come to you as a river, I bring forth much life. It is I who carries you in my courageous current. With little motion you rise to the top. I carry you through constant changing conditions to remind you that your comfort is not in your condition but in mine. Your Savior, filled with mercy and grace, is your flotation device, for without it you would be sucked under the strong currents. Extend my grace to others and always look into the deep to draw out what you can love. Everyone can be loved and is in need. Teach others to give love outrageously and you will see changed lives and hearts and souls.

*"And above all things have fervent love for one another, for "love will cover a multitude of sins." (1 Peter 4:8)*

*"A new commandment I give to you, that you love one another; as I have loved you, that you also love one another." (John 13:34)*

*"Owe no one anything except to love one another, for he who loves another has fulfilled the law." (Romans 13:8)*

## The Way, the Truth, the Life

Producing my palpable placements;

   Pressing pounds of products,

      Planting peace in dry pastures, and

         Sowing seed in fertile soil:

I *bring* what I am—LIFE;

   I *give* what I am—TRUTH;

      I *show* what I am—THE WAY!

*"Jesus said to him, "I am the way, the truth, and the life. No one comes to the Father except through me." (John 14:6)*

No one has life without me for a flower separated from the vine will surely die. No one knows the truth without knowing me for I am truth. If I am not within, how can one know me and experience truth? If you walk not with me, you walk not with truth, for I am truth.

## The Door of Self

If I tell you I am the door—that no one comes to the Father but by me, then truly, truthfully I am.

*"Jesus said to him, "I am the way, the truth, and the life. No one comes to the Father except through me." (John 14:6)*

**If there were another door, I would have told you.**

*"I am the door. If anyone enters by me, he will be saved, and will go in and out and find pasture." (John 10:9)*

Behind the door of self and through the dark quest for light is a brick wall leading to nowhere but the dungeon of

Self-reliance,

   Self-promotion, and

      Self-exaltation—all leading to failure and self-pity.

I am the lamp unto your feet; follow me and your path will be lit and straight.

> *"Thy word is a lamp unto my feet, and a light unto my path."* (Psalm 119:105 KJV)

> *"For this is he that was spoken of by the prophet Esaias, saying, The voice of one crying in the wilderness, Prepare ye the way of the Lord, make his paths straight."* (Matthew 3:3)

Go and be about your Father's business as I am and walk in the fullness of joy for peace abounds and my mercy endures forever.

> *"Oh, give thanks to the LORD, for He is good! For His mercy endures forever."* (1 Chronicles 16:34)

## A Challenge to a Young Man

You cannot outrun sin—you cannot hide from the shame it brings. Just confess it to me and I will be faithful to cleanse you.

> *"If we confess our sins, He is faithful and just to forgive us our sins and to cleanse us from all unrighteousness."* (1 John 1:9)

I will bring you into victory if you will only surrender to me. Stop now all bad choices and allow me to direct you.

*"In all your ways acknowledge him, and he shall direct your paths."* (Proverbs 3:6)

Do not make decisions to cover up other bad decisions. Just let my love drive fear from you and do not allow pride to bring you to a fall.

*"Pride goes before destruction and a haughty spirit before a fall."* (Proverbs 16:18)

What I have revealed about your future will not come to pass without your cooperation, so take heed and know that I am God—nothing is impossible with me.

*"But Jesus looked at them and said to them, "With men this is impossible, but with God all things are possible."* (Matthew 19:26)

In your own strength you will fall, but in me and with me, you will find life to the full, pressed down and overflowing.

*"Give, and it will be given to you: good measure, pressed down, shaken together, and running over will be put into your bosom. For with the same measure that you use, it will be measured back to you."* (Luke 6:38)

You have ignored certain godly wisdom. Do you not know that I have sent many messengers?

*"The wise men are ashamed; they are dismayed and taken. Behold, they have rejected the word of the LORD; so what wisdom do they have?"* (Jeremiah 8:9)

My will is to prosper your soul, not to damage it. Come to me; sit with me alone and allow my instruction. I will give you rest and peace and will guide your direction.

*"Come to me, all you who labor and are heavy laden, and I will give you rest."* (Matthew 11:28)

Do not jump too soon; just pray and I will answer your need. Peace be with you, my child. I do not condemn you; you have condemned yourself.

*"Happy is he who does not condemn himself in what he approves."* (Romans 14:22b)

I offer life and freedom and victory in every way. Live well and follow my design. Do not judge yourself so harshly.

*"Judge not, and you shall not be judged. Condemn not, and you shall not be condemned. Forgive, and you will be forgiven."* (Luke 6:37)

Everything I am and everything I do is from love, for I am love. I bless you—turn to me and see.

*"And we have known and believed the love that God has for us. God is love, and he who abides in love abides in God, and God in him."* (1 John 4:16)

*July 25th*

**Don't Worry**

Just relax and enjoy my blessings. Don't worry about anything.

> *"Therefore do not worry about tomorrow, for tomorrow will worry about its own things."* (Matthew 6:34)

Your business is in my hands. Your very life hangs in the balance of my sovereignty. Bind all infirmity and loose perfect love and peace upon your house and sickness will not stand. Be mindful of my presence with you.

> *"And I will give you the keys of the kingdom of heaven, and whatever you bind on earth will be bound in heaven, and whatever you loose on earth will be loosed in heaven."* (Matthew 16:19)

# July 26th

**Rest in Me**

All who come to me with good intentions will find rest and be filled with life for I see in the deep places of every heart.

> *"Take my yoke upon you and learn from me, for I am gentle and lowly in heart, and you will find rest for your souls."* (Matthew 11:29)

Rest in knowing it is I who has prepared provision.

> *"And my God shall supply all your need according to his riches in glory by Christ Jesus."* (Philippians 4:19)

Do not worry about what has not yet come to pass. Focus on just the next step. You are doing well and I am with you in every way. When you slip from faith to doubt or doubt to discouragement, remember it is I who cause success.

> *"So Jesus answered and said to them, "Assuredly, I say to you, if you have faith and do not doubt, you will not only do what was done to the fig tree, but also if you say to this mountain, 'Be removed and be cast into the sea,' it will be done."* (Mathew 21:21)

It's time to rest in me and not to be in worry. Do not fear!

> *"And the LORD appeared to him the same night and said, "I am the God of your father Abraham; do not fear, for I am with you."* (Genesis 26:24)

# *July 27th*

## Be on Guard

Peace be with you, my lovely child. Be on guard and alert for the battle that rises against you has come to unsettle your mind. I have prepared great rewards to encourage you to follow the path I have laid at your feet. Keep focused but also stay relaxed. Be dependent and disciplined.

> *"But I discipline my body and bring it into subjection, lest, when I have preached to others, I myself should become disqualified."*
> (1 Corinthians 9:27)

I am releasing a prosperous portion.

## Twelve Pillars

Twelve pillars represent my foundation of strength—all relying on each other to uphold my purpose, bearing each other's burdens that together I have caused to be light. Not one pillar could possibly bear the weight on its own, but all are needed to support the foundation in a different area. Listen very carefully to my directions and I will lead you perfectly by my Spirit as you submit full to my will.

*"And the LORD went before them by day in a pillar of cloud to lead the way, and by night in a pillar of fire to give them light, so as to go by day and night."* (Exodus 13:21)

*"And Moses wrote all the words of the LORD. And he rose early in the morning, and built an altar at the foot of the mountain, and twelve pillars according to the twelve tribes of Israel."* (Exodus 24:4)

*"He who overcomes, I will make him a pillar in the temple of my God, and he shall go out no more. I will write on him the name of my God and the name of the city of My God, the New Jerusalem, which comes down out of heaven from My God. And I will write on him my new name."* (Revelation 3:12)

## Thank You

Thank you for what you have done, and thank you for what I see you doing in the upcoming months. I am pleased with what I see. Love and teach love and you will see transformation and abundance in every way. Glory is increasing toward heaven and heaven smiles on those who walk with kingdom awareness. Continue your faithful service. Release upon those I show you, and grant grace to those who speak against you.

*"Therefore they stayed there a long time, speaking boldly in the Lord, who was bearing witness to the word of His grace, granting signs and wonders to be done by their hands."* (Acts 14:3)

Be merciful and you will receive much more mercy.

*"Therefore be merciful, just as your Father also is merciful."* (Luke 6:36)

# July 30th

**Encouragement for the Lord's Day**

Do as I ask today; prepare your heart for my increase. Do not be afraid—my plan is perfect. Today will be a great day for The Rock of the Harbor. Let my Spirit lead you and listen for my voice. I know you hear me—I have willed it so. Those who have ears to hear, let them hear.

*"If anyone has ears to hear, let him hear!"* (Mark 7:16)

Those who have eyes to see, let them see the goodness of a gracious King.

*"Son of man, look with your eyes and hear with your ears, and fix your mind on everything I show you."* (Ezekiel 40:4)

Walk in love and obey my commands. Be balanced in grace and law, and receive all that I have to give.

*"For the law was given through Moses, but grace and truth came through Jesus Christ."* (John 1:17)

Never give up on what I have revealed about your destiny. Do not allow guilt and condemnation to bring weight to your ankles—I have made you free.

> *"For the law of the Spirit of life in Christ Jesus has made me free from the law of sin and death."* (Romans 8:2)

Let those who are imprisoned push out of their own cages. I have unlocked the door to abundance and restoration. Be ye not deceived; there is no bondage that can hold you down when you walk in closeness to me. I am that I am and I will!

## A Lord's Day Critique

*I always look forward to sitting with the Lord after the Sunday service at The Rock to see what he has to say about it.*

You did a great job listening to my instruction. I am still touching those who came in a special way. There was so much ground laid, even more than necessary, but nevertheless I will water every seed. To live and love outrageously is a great topic of immeasurable importance. I will increase your anointing as you continue in obedience to me. Spend more time with me this week and meditate on my Word and I will speak to you besides. There is no mountain too high; there is no promise too great that I cannot deliver.

I will give you your place of refuge;

I will give you heaven opened because

I have seen you in quiet;

I have heard the cries from deep within you;

I have seen you believe when no evidence was outwardly confirmed.

You are magnificent in my sight and I admire what I have made. You will receive, pressed down and spilling over.

*"Give and it will be given to you: good measure, pressed down, shaken together, and running over will be put into your bosom. For with the same measure that you use, it will be measured back to you."* (Luke 6:38)

Gracious and loving I smile upon you as I reflect on your service today. Well done, my child—well done!

## Armed and Dangerous

Great is your strength in me and forward my angels march along beside you. Always be aware that you are not alone—the armies of hell cannot prevail against you.

*"On this rock I will build my church, and the gates of hell shall not prevail against it."* (Matthew 16:18)

You are armed and dangerous with weapons of mass destruction toward the camps of the Enemy. I will raise you from ashes to free the captives of religious pride and performance. You do not need to study the doctrines of man—just the ways of Jesus and you will have what hell fears.

*"And in vain they worship me, teaching as doctrines the commandments of men."* (Matthew 15:9)

*"Now the Spirit expressly says that in latter times some will depart from the faith, giving heed to deceiving spirits and doctrines of demons."* (1 Timothy 4:1)

*"Do not be carried about with various and strange doctrines. For it is good that the heart be established by grace, not with foods which have not profited those who have been occupied with them."* (Hebrews 13:9)

## Trip the Traps

Plans are being raised against you and I continue to trip the traps. I laugh as I see deceptions exposed.

*"He who sits in the heavens shall laugh; The Lord shall hold them in derision."* (Psalm 2:4)

I have used your mouth to liberate; I will cause your mind to be increasingly sharp. Get on and ride the white horse of righteousness—your defender has fit the saddle. What was made for you cannot be taken away. I love your tears of joy that you cry from longing. I love your faith when friends rise against you and you bless them back in the face of evil.

August 2011

# August 2nd

The Lord woke me at 3:33 a.m.[1], saying he wanted to speak to me. I hurried downstairs, lit a fire, plunked myself down on the couch, and started writing.

## False Judgment

Do not allow yourself to be discouraged. Much good has resulted in your willingness to pursue me, even against all odds. Do not admit you are wrong in areas of obedience or you will solidify false judgment.

> *"They have spoken words, swearing falsely in making a covenant. Thus judgment springs up like hemlock in the furrows of the field."* (Hosea 10:4)

You obeyed me to start The Rock of the Harbor and have been judged harshly for your obedience. Why then do some speak from bitterness against you? Is it because they cannot control you? I am your pilot and the captain of your craft. Will the results speak for themselves?

---

1 The number 333 has many special meanings for me, one being the verse at Jeremiah 33:3 "Call to me and I will answer you and show you great and mighty things which you do not know." The Lord used this verse to pique my curiosity to follow him on this great adventure.

Continue on and invite all to join you—even those who attempt to speak against you. Love all as if they were your own and I will deal with them. You will not need to set any straight. Your job is just to obey me.

*"Now therefore, if you will indeed obey my voice and keep my covenant, then you shall be a special treasure to me above all people; for all the earth is mine."* (Exodus 19:5)

This time of transition is exciting, and I see that you have eager expectation. I am pleased with your attitude. Although most are expecting you to fail, when success is what they see, they will come. I am your defender; if you are close to me, you have safety.

## Jesus Sits Down with Me

*I felt the presence of the Lord and looked to see where he was. He appeared in the Spirit right next to me, and then sat down. Even though he appeared transparent, I could tell he was about 5'11" with blue eyes sparking like water, long brown wavy hair, and a short kept beard. A long white robe covered his body and was wrapped with a blue sash. The hair on my arms stood on end and my body tingled, head to toe, from the power of his presence, and even though I was sitting, my body felt weightless.*

I just sat down with you—can you feel my presence?

*Yes.*

Do you know why I have come?

*No.*

Because I remind you with my presence that you are not alone—I am with you. You will endure more persecution, but I am with you. Behold I make all things new.

*Jesus, the Prince of Peace, shows me a peace sign. He touched my knee and said,*

I bless you—I bless you.

*Then he pointed to a huge white angel standing before the fireplace, and when I looked, the angel smiled and stretched out his wings. That angel was joined by another and then one angel after another....Goose bumps ran up and down my body! "How many are there, Lord?" Pointing around the room, he showed me all the angels; then he looked at me again and said,*

There are twelve.

*Wow! Is this for real or is this my imagination?*

It is as real as my Spirit. I have allowed you to see into a realm of heaven, and now you are able to see increasingly in the Spirit. Do not tell everyone what you see, only those whom I show you.[2]

*I looked around the room again and I saw one of the twelve angels put out his wings three times as if to say, "Here I am."*

You will be a target, but I will protect you to fulfill your destiny. Let yourself rest in me; let yourself be comforted. Allow me to train you in my ways. I have appointed many to come and my Spirit is releasing. The weight is on me, although I remain weightless. The joy in me is full and so you too must laugh often.

*"You will show me the path of life; In Your presence is fullness of joy; At Your right hand are pleasures forevermore."* (Psalm 16:11)

---

2 There are many instances in Scripture where the Lord says, "Tell no one...." As in Mark 9:9. It's a matter of timing: what is not right to tell at one time is right to tell at another. Now is the time to tell this story.

Release my life through your laughter; teach others to laugh at fear and their own failures—laugh with faith-filled anticipation.

> *"Then our mouth was filled with laughter, and our tongue with singing. Then they said among the nations, "The LORD has done great things for them."* (Psalm 126:2)

Be not afraid, for I am with you, as you can see. I approached you again from the East.

*He touched my head again and said:*

I bless you. I do not tire of watching you—I study your every move. Walking in love toward everyone is my call to contagious Christianity. Do this in remembrance of me. You are on the journey of a lifetime and I am here. You will not fail because I am here. You will give yourself away and gain loves barrier breaker. Remember, there are no borders in my kingdom. I have written my wisdom on your heart—not so you would be prideful, but that you would hear. The Holy Spirit, whispers to you and you hear, softly sending my message to your ear so you will know direction from heaven. Do what you see me do and be prepared to go when I send you. You can be in perfect peace in the center of a tornado. If you stay in the center of my will, you will stay in peace. If peace departs from you, adjust your position and it will be restored to you.

These things that I say to you will bless many and are going to be imparted in print for others to glean. I show you movement in the room, and you sense my Holy presence. I radiate around you. Do you feel my love?

*Yes, Lord.*

Be still and know that nothing is impossible with me.

Dare to believe;

Dare to receive;

Dare to step out on faith and see me cover you.

I provide for every step and I bring them to your feet.

*Where will I stay, Lord? (I'm referring to where I will live.)*

You will stay with me and I with you; then I will shine a light unto your feet and you will see clearly through the dark.

> *"Thy word is a lamp unto my feet, and a light unto my path."* (Psalm 119:105)

## Faith Is What I Require

Showing you the stages is fun for me; I enjoy seeing you exercise faith, and faith is what I require. I need your faith to be increasingly strong so I answer you like this, "Wait and see." I will show you that confidence should not be in your plan but in mine. How much more will your faith grow when I test it?

> *"My brethren, count it all joy when you fall into various trials, knowing that the testing of your faith produces patience."* (James 1:2-3)

I am waiting for the last minute to allow for your improved faith. Do you not see that you are heavily guarded? (Twelve angels are about the house and property.) How much more then will I provide a place of rest? Give me praise for what I have done although you do not yet see—this is the secret to releasing faith in what is hoped for.

*"Now faith is the substance of things hoped for, the evidence of things not seen."* (Hebrews 11:1)

I delight in your willingness to give me your time. Share this secret with others and I will change their lives also, for I am going to bring a revolution. Get your thoughts in perfect order and prepare them as if you were setting a table for very important guests, and I will bring food from heaven, and you will feast upon all that is good. There is a time to feast and a time to fast.

Wellspring be filled,

    Pour from me—living water,

        Bringing abundant life from the Rock.

*In a vision, I saw a man, then another and another—twelve total, sitting at a table with Jesus who was breaking bread and passing it out to his disciples, saying, "One of you will betray me." Then I heard my song playing:*

## Which One Will Betray You?

*Verse:*
He stood up to the testing;
His life He was investing;
He said one of us will
Betray Him before morn.
Who could it be, standing here with me;
Is it I, Lord—oh, is it I?

*Chorus:*
Which one will betray you?
Which one will betray you?
Which one will betray you before morn?

Which one will deny you?
Which one will stand beside you?
Which one will betray you before morn?

*Verse:*
Though we all had good intensions
Our hearts were weak and poor;
We saw miracles time and time again.
He said He'd have to die;
We asked him, Lord why?
He said it'd give us power over sin.

*Pre Chorus:*
Which one will betray you?
Is it I? Is it I?
Which one will betray you?
Is it I? Is it I? Is it I?

*Chorus (C-part):*
I know I'm far from perfect;
Lord, how could it be
That I could ever betray you
After all you've done for me?

*Jesus got up from the couch where he was sitting and left the room. Later in the day, he said:*

All that I am and all that I do is from love. Remain in me and I will remain in you. A heart that is surrendered to me is a heart that is filled.

# August 3rd

## Your Time is the Greatest Gift

Do you know how I care for you?

> *"Casting all your care upon him; for he careth for you."*
> (1 Peter 5:7 KJV)

Do you know how I long for the time you give me? If you were to give me any of all gifts, your time would be the most valuable. I am surrounding you with goodness.

> *"Then He said, "I will make all my goodness pass before you, and I will proclaim the name of the LORD before you. I will be gracious to whom I will be gracious, and I will have compassion on whom I will have compassion."* (Exodus 33:19)

I am lavishing you with heavenly gifts. I am sending messages out on your behalf. I have defended you among the nations. I have danced upon distress, and it has dissipated daunting distractions.

## Renew Your Mind

I desire to renew your mind and give you supernatural sharpness.

> *"And do not be conformed to this world, but be transformed by the renewing of your mind, that you may prove what is that good and acceptable and perfect will of God."* (Romans 12:2)

When you weigh my call against selfishness, you see weightless proportion. Provisions are palpable and produce preparation principles. Get good gracious gratitude ready for your ship of goods has pulled into the harbor. Pick up what I put down and peacefully prepare. No shadow can corner your focused mind. No doubt can steal your tune. Guard your heart.

> *"Be anxious for nothing, but in everything by prayer and supplication, with thanksgiving, let your requests be made known to God; and the peace of God, which surpasses all understanding, will guard your hearts and minds through Christ Jesus."* (Philippians 4:6-7)

# August 6th

## Well Done

Well done! Well done! Well done! My best is best and getting better. You have done well to lead in trusting me—great is your reward. You have rested in faith, and I intend to reward all faithfulness. Enter into my courts with thanksgiving and abundant praise and offer unto me all your hopes and dreams and I will shower them with provision.

*"For the kingdom of heaven is like a man traveling to a far country, who called his own servants and delivered his goods to them. And to one he gave five talents, to another two, and to another one, to each according to his own ability; and immediately he went on a journey. Then he who had received the five talents went and traded with them, and made another five talents. And likewise he who had received two gained two more also. But he who had received one went and dug in the ground, and hid his lord's money. After a long time the lord of those servants came and settled accounts with them. "So he who had received five talents came and brought five other talents, saying, 'Lord, you delivered to me five talents; look, I have gained five more talents besides them.' His lord said to him, 'Well done, good and faithful servant; you were faithful over a few things,*

*I will make you ruler over many things. Enter into the joy of your lord.' He also who had received two talents came and said, 'Lord, you delivered to me two talents; look, I have gained two more talents besides them.' His lord said to him, 'Well done, good and faithful servant; you have been faithful over a few things, I will make you ruler over many things. Enter into the joy of your lord.' "Then he who had received the one talent came and said, 'Lord, I knew you to be a hard man, reaping where you have not sown, and gathering where you have not scattered seed. And I was afraid, and went and hid your talent in the ground. Look, there you have what is yours.' "But his lord answered and said to him, 'You wicked and lazy servant, you knew that I reap where I have not sown, and gather where I have not scattered seed. So you ought to have deposited my money with the bankers, and at my coming I would have received back my own with interest. Therefore take the talent from him, and give it to him who has ten talents. 'For to everyone who has, more will be given, and he will have abundance; but from him who does not have, even what he has will be taken away. And cast the unprofitable servant into the outer darkness. There will be weeping and gnashing of teeth.'"* (Matthew 25:14-30)

## Family Reunion

This is an important day for the family. This reunion is special, and this family is very important to me. Love them, and show grace and acceptance and interest. I'm proud of you and what I see in your changing personality. You no longer spend your time convincing others of your importance because you have accepted what I have said about you. Do you feel my presence with you? I have observed your behavior closely, and I have given you revelation. You are not a common man because I have called you to kingdom transformation.

Liberate—

Evaluate—

Do not deviate—

My plan is perfect and every detail has been calculated from heaven. Walk closely in every thought.

## A Shaking

The ground will be shaken, but you will not be removed. I am preparing my manifestation of power, and many will rethink their life courses. Do not be troubled by this word [of the coming shaking]. I will shout my plan to your soul, and you will hear beyond what you have yet encountered.

## Seducers

Be on guard for the seducers—many will come as I increase your anointing—

Women,

The world systems, and

Those hungry for power and attention.

*"I know your works, love, service, faith, and your patience; and as for your works, the last are more than the first. Nevertheless I have a few things against you, because you allow that woman Jezebel, who calls herself a prophetess, to teach and seduce my servants to commit sexual immorality and eat things sacrificed to idols."* (Revelation 2:19-21)

Focus yourself completely on me in everything you do and you will have safety. Be on guard and love outrageously. Every step has been measured, and I see the results. My smile is pointed toward you, and my face shines upon you because you have a bold heart, like that of a lion with uncommon fearlessness and a powerful tongue that speaks from the deep.

Give me your thoughts and I will perfect them;

Give me your dreams and I will collect them;

Be pleased in me as I am pleased in you.

Get what I speak and apply my life

For you have been given the keys to my kingdom.

## The Fields Are Prepared

Jump and run with playful anticipation and you will see the fields I have prepared for you:

Some to sow,

Some to plow,

Some to enjoy and watch grow, and

Some to eat from and be nourished by.

Everything I give is a reminder of my presence with you. I show you what exists in the Spirit because seeing in the Spirit will be necessary for you.

*"And it shall come to pass in the last days, says God, That I will pour out of my Spirit on all flesh; Your sons and your daughters shall*

*prophesy, Your young men shall see visions, Your old men shall dream dreams."* (Acts 2:17)

Continue as I have shown and remember what I have promised. It is not the end but the beginning cycle of what I have made you to be. Remember that every move you make should be a result of time spent with me.

Keep trusting,

Keep loving, and

Keep extending mercy.

Never forget that it is I who directs your going.

Gather now what has been sown!

## Mt. Rainier

It's good that you climbed it when you did. Mt. Rainier is going to blow its top, and many will receive warnings to evacuate; many who do not receive warnings will be killed. It will not be sudden. It will be televised and evacuation processes will be followed by the masses. Many homes will be destroyed along with roads and buildings. River ways will be disastrous, and more opportunity for salvation will be the result. Sin has taken more lives than natural disasters, but disasters are a result of the judgment of sin.

# August 8th

**Surrender Anxious Thoughts**

I want you to surrender all of your anxious thoughts to me.

> *"Be anxious for nothing, but in everything by prayer and supplication, with thanksgiving, let your requests be made known to God; and the peace of God, which surpasses all understanding, will guard your hearts and minds through Christ Jesus."* (Philippians 4:6-7)

It is I who am guiding your very breath and the details of your life are my focus. Too many people think it is easy to die to self, but self dies hard—it takes practice and time.

> *"What shall we say then? Shall we continue in sin that grace may abound? Certainly not! How shall we who died to sin live any longer in it? Or do you not know that as many of us as were baptized into Christ Jesus were baptized into his death?"* (Romans 6:1-3)

Continue taking time to practice and I will show you new ways to serve and to become selfless. Do not be concerned at areas of failure; just work on the areas in which you are led by my Spirit to improve.

## Spend Time with the Prince

Peace rules the peacemaker, and the peacemaker stays in peace when he spends time with the prince.

> *"Blessed are the peacemakers, for they shall be called sons of God."* (Matthew 5:9)

Do not grow weary of doing good, for doing good is the secret to satisfaction, and satisfied you will be.

> *"And let us not grow weary while doing good, for in due season we shall reap if we do not lose heart."* (Galatians 6:9)

Do not ignore your past discipline—remember that I discipline those I love and call my sons.

> *"But I discipline my body and bring it into subjection, lest, when I have preached to others, I myself should become disqualified."* (1 Corinthians 9:27)

Obedience curbs my discipline and selflessness redirects my wrath.

> *"Do you not know that to whom you present yourselves slaves to obey, you are that one's slaves whom you obey, whether of sin leading to death, or of obedience leading to righteousness?"* (Romans 6:16)

I do not desire to punish you, but I will if necessary, so do as I say and simply obey.

> *"Observe and obey all these words which I command you, that it may go well with you and your children after you forever, when you do what is good and right in the sight of the LORD your God."* (Deuteronomy 12:28)

You hear my instruction; there is no need to adopt the doubt of others.

> *"So Jesus answered and said to them, "Assuredly, I say to you, if you have faith and do not doubt, you will not only do what was done to the fig tree, but also if you say to this mountain, 'be removed and be cast into the sea,' it will be done."* (Matthew 21:21)

My voice is strong in you and I will carry out my purpose. Meditate on my word day and night.

> *"This Book of the Law shall not depart from your mouth, but you shall meditate in it day and night, that you may observe to do according to all that is written in it. For then you will make your way prosperous, and then you will have good success."* (Joshua 1:8)

I will construct your message.

Be still,

Recall, and

Consider

That I am still on the throne calling the shots. You don't need to control anything; just let me rule and reign and you will be in complete peace.

> *"You will keep him in perfect peace, whose mind is stayed on you, because he trusts in you."* (Isaiah 26:3)

# August 16th

## Prepare Your Mind

One by one, you have dared to believe, and I will reward your faith, pressed down, shaken together, and running over.

> *"Give, and it will be given to you: good measure, pressed down, shaken together, and running over will be put into your bosom. For with the same measure that you use, it will be measured back to you."* (Luke 6:38)

Continue to share my love and be ready—the anointing of my Spirit is being increased to a level fit for abounding breakthrough. Well done at passing the test of your faith and faithfulness.

> *"My brethren, count it all joy when you fall into various trials, knowing that the testing of your faith produces patience. But let patience have its perfect work, that you may be perfect and complete, lacking nothing."* (James 1:2-4)

Hold out your hands and let it spill over. The heavens have opened unto you that my glory would be fully manifest. Lay down your memories of past trials and prepare your mind to receive the abundance of my kingdom. I will pour through your willingness.

*"But the wisdom that is from above is first pure, then peaceable, gentle, willing to yield, full of mercy and good fruits, without partiality and without hypocrisy."* (James 3:17)

Get what I am giving while my giving abounds so no one can miss my hand's motion. Swing in favor toward destiny's song and allow yourself to sing with new resolution.

## Abundance

Do you know of what I am speaking? Abundance in every area of your outrageous life that draws people to the same desire to seek my face as you have previously shown. Well done, my servant. You have reaped only the beginning of what you have sown.

*"Now may He who supplies seed to the sower, and bread for food, supply and multiply the seed you have sown and increase the fruits of your righteousness."* (2 Corinthians 9:10)

*"Do not be deceived, God is not mocked; for whatever a man sows, that he will also reap for he who sows to his flesh will of the flesh reap corruption, but he who sows to the Spirit will of the Spirit reap everlasting life."* (Galatians 6:7)

Gather the gatherers, for you will need much help. Your ever-increasing boldness will ring hearts back to the beating of the drum of heaven that unlocks the dead.

Wake up my sleeping church, beloved!

Wake up my selfish bride!

Do not let your riches steer you from righteousness, but let righteousness steer your riches.

*"I love those who love me, and those who seek me diligently will find me. Riches and honor are with me—enduring riches and righteousness."* (Proverbs 8:17-18)

## Give Away the Bread of Life

Fill my house with the hurting and the hungry, and then give away the Bread of Life.

*"And Jesus said to them, 'I am the bread of life. He who comes to me shall never hunger, and he who believes in me shall never thirst."* (John 6:35)

Provide a way for the wayward,

Pave the way for the hopeless,

Restore my broken, and

Rest in my holiness—that grace would abound.

Goodness and mercy shall follow you all of your days, and will rock this nation with the love that has unreservedly filled you.

*"Surely goodness and mercy shall follow me all the days of my life; and I will dwell in the house of the LORD forever."* (Psalm 23:6)

Reach continually to the heavens and I will hand you every key to every door, and nothing shall be impossible.

*"And I will give you the keys of the kingdom of heaven, and whatever you bind on earth will be bound in heaven, and whatever you loose on earth will be loosed in heaven."* (Matthew 16:19)

Your faith has brought a fragrance to my nostrils and a smile to my face.

I have reached out my hand to you and you see it—

I have called and you have come—

I have sent you and you go—with eagerness and full expectation.

## My Grace Abounds

Let your disappointments fall like the demons sent to destroy you, and rise to the occasion of mercy.

> *"But God, who is rich in mercy, because of his great love with which he loved us, even when we were dead in trespasses, made us alive together with Christ (by grace you have been saved), and raised us up together, and made us sit together in the heavenly places in Christ Jesus, that in the ages to come he might show the exceeding riches of his grace in his kindness toward us in Christ Jesus."* (Ephesians 2:4-7)

My grace abounds beyond your ability to sin. You have chosen to dive into my divinity; therefore, you will carry the fruit of plenty to bless those who humble themselves and ask of you, so that every need is met. Heaven is handing you a prosperous portion of favor that cannot be stopped from motion. Expect what I have said and waver not, for there is no time for uncertainty.

## The Battle Has Been Won

The battle has been won. Walk the walk; fight the good fight like the victor you have become, brave heart surrendered to me.

*"Fight the good fight. This charge I commit to you, son Timothy, according to the prophecies previously made concerning you, that by them you may wage the good warfare."* (1 Timothy 1:18)

If only you knew what a threat you are to the powers of darkness. If only you knew how much warring has taken place on your behalf. Finish well. I see you in paradise, smiling at the journey of your long life.

# August 17th

**Hearing Wrong?**

Don't be discouraged about hearing wrong. Remember that it is possible to hear the voice of your own desires. When *you* would like something to happen *is* always NOW—but my timing is perfect. Be patient as I am patient and I will prompt you at the right time.

> *"The end of a thing is better than its beginning; the patient in spirit is better than the proud in spirit."* (Ecclesiastes 7:8)

> *"And a servant of the Lord must not quarrel but be gentle to all, able to teach, patient, in humility correcting those who are in opposition, if God perhaps will grant them repentance, so that they may know the truth and that they may come to their senses and escape the snare of the devil, having been taken captive by him to do his will."* (2 Timothy 2:23-26)

Never stop believing for my best:

Keep the faith;

Keep your courage;

Never give up;

Be of good cheer; and

Don't allow discouragement.

You have passed many tests!

# August 18th

## Keep Seeking Me

Keep seeking me in your thoughts. Collect them carefully as if you are sorting. Hold on to what is pure; quickly disregard what is not, and you will know the secret in increasing your ability to house my anointing.

> *"Finally, brethren, whatever things are true, whatever things are noble, whatever things are just, whatever things are pure, whatever things are lovely, whatever things are of good report, if there is any virtue and if there is anything praiseworthy—meditate on these things."* (Philippians 4:8)

> *"To the pure all things are pure, but to those who are defiled and unbelieving nothing is pure; but even their mind and conscience are defiled."* (Titus 1:15)

Walk always by faith, not by sight.

> *"For we walk by faith, not by sight."* (2 Corinthians 5:7)

## The Battle Rages

Remember that the battle rages around you, and the Enemy is strategizing a way to cause you to fall, so keep me first in every way and know that I am fully with you.

> *"Be sober, be vigilant; because your adversary the devil walks about like a roaring lion, seeking whom he may devour."* (1 Peter 5:8)

## The Call

Do not lose sight of the call I have clearly defined. This is not a game of make believe. You are on a mission from heaven, and I will give you clear instruction, so listen carefully.

When you sense that I am cautioning you,

> Be cautioned;

When I am giving you a sense to move forward,

> Move with boldness;

When I am speaking to you about someone,

> Share only what I prompt you to.

Give hope and life and peace

> through the encouragement I have put inside of you.

> *"For you can all prophesy one by one, that all may learn and all may be encouraged."* (1 Corinthians 14:31)

# August 20th

## The Perfect Message

*The Lord is teaching me how to preach. Do you think it will pass as a homiletics class?*

Remember that I am with you. Having an idea about what to say—according to my will, is enough. You may feel a need to prepare the perfect message, but the perfect message is born of my Spirit and is released by faith. Have faith that I am bringing the message and that it is filled with love and grace.

- Speak about the armor and the call to battle.

- Speak about love.

- Speak about the need to spend time with me.

- Share of your experience in quiet times.

- Talk about hunger for me which is the activator.

- Talk about what I have revealed by my Spirit and the movement that is coming (the swirl and the heart of love equipping center).

- Talk about favor linked to obedience.

- Do all that my Spirit leads you to do.

# August 22nd

**Retaliation**

You are experiencing some retaliation from your victory yesterday, but I am settling your mind.

> *"Behold, I will raise them out of the place to which you have sold them, and will return your retaliation upon your own head."* (Joel 3:4)

Rest in me and know that I am not your thoughts but their director.

**Well Done**

Well done yesterday. I paid a visit to The Rock of the Harbor and I was so pleased. I bless you. You are increasing in capacity to house me.

**Pride**

Pride has many forms and is subtle—

Sneaky as the serpent, it wraps itself around the rejected

To bring false security and false worth.

Identity, rooted in me,

Brings freedom through understanding, and

Humility is the result.

# August 25th

## Lay Down Your Life

Get your diet on course;

   Get your exercise dialed in;

      Spend time with me like this alone often and

         I tell you that you cannot fail.

Remember that no greater is any man than he who lays down his life for another. Lay down your life for me, as I have done for you, and teach my ways of sacrifice. Serve others and instruct those who watch you to be a servant to all—for what does it profit a man simply to be served?

> *"For even the Son of Man did not come to be served, but to serve, and to give his life a ransom for many."* (Mark 10:45)

## The Tempting

There is a time and place that is scheduled for your tempting—so be being filled with my Spirit, and run away from the evil into victory, and I will allow you to prevail against the schemes of the Destroyer.

*"Therefore do not be unwise, but understand what the will of the Lord is. And do not be drunk with wine, in which is dissipation; but be filled with the Spirit, speaking to one another in psalms and hymns and spiritual songs, singing and making melody in your heart to the Lord, giving thanks always for all things to God the Father in the name of our Lord Jesus Christ, submitting to one another in the fear of God."* (Ephesians 5:17-21)

Be on guard, for as you increase in my holiness so will the forces of darkness try to stop you. Be sharp in your mind and quick with your sword to fight against what is sent to disrupt my order.

*"For the word of God is living and powerful, and sharper than any two-edged sword, piercing even to the division of soul and spirit, and of joints and marrow, and is a discerner of the thoughts and intents of the heart."* (Hebrews 4:12)

You will be victorious, for I have already seen your responses. Get your Scriptures hung on your wall and begin the memorization. I will show you which ones to print. Learn them well because they will be needed.

## Your Business

Your business is my business and my business is always a winner.

I am the Rock of your Salvation—the Prince,

Where no darkness can hide;

The lover of your soul, and

The preparer of your long-term best interests.

I am picking up the pieces of your past and creating something beautiful for your future.

**Waves**

Do not be concerned with waves—just keep your eyes on me and others will not be able to deny my abundance. What does not bear fruit will be cut off, and what bears fruit will be food to many.

> *"Every branch in me that does not bear fruit he takes away; and every branch that bears fruit he prunes, that it may bear more fruit."* (John 15:2)

Continue, my child, to bear fruit and feed many. Go now and do as I have said.

Work out,

    Feed your Spirit,

        Allow me to direct you in business,

            Memorize my Word, and

                Walk in purity.

# August 26th

**The Course of Victory**

Get your mind set on the course of victory.

  Doubt sees impossibility;

    Faith sees only that which is possible.

      Hope for substance, and

        Evidence your faith.

When you see a wall, I see a door;

  When you run out of strength, I exercise my will.

    Rest in me and work from there.

Remember that your mind is where the seeds live.

  Let others' discouragements motivate encouragement and

    Lean not on what limits your perspective

      But on my principle of peace.

Ride the back of promise and don't be kicked off!

*"Now faith is the substance of things hoped for, the evidence of things not seen."* (Hebrews 11:1)

*"Trust in the LORD with all your heart, and lean not on your own understanding."* (Proverbs 3:5)

*"And this is the promise that He has promised us—eternal life."* (1 John 2:25)

## Pride Destroys Unity

True unity is learned in a culture where each body member learns to die to self. Working together means shelving pride and ego; the biggest destroyer of unity is pride.

*"A man's pride will bring him low, but the humble in spirit will retain honor."* (Proverbs 29:23)

*"The pride of your heart has deceived you, you who dwell in the clefts of the rock, whose habitation is high; you who say in your heart, 'Who will bring me down to the ground?'"* (Obadiah 1:3)

Pride wants to be exalted and worshiped, which is why some worship teams have become so ineffective—because they are performance-driven and seek audience worship and approval. My true worshipers have a focus on who I am as Lord and praise with an appreciation of my love and mercy in all that I've done for them.

## A Gift or an Office?

There are times when I, the Lord your God, temporarily assign many areas of gifting for the purpose of leadership and equipping with broader understanding. A teacher may be anointed and then appointed to teach only or to have more than one position. I want you to learn the difference between having a gift and holding the office of that gift. There will continue to be some specific instructions I give to you only for the purpose of overseer. I am and will continue to broaden your understanding of Church polity and show you what I want corrected in the preparation of my bride.

*I had a vision of a beautiful bride needing adjustment before she walked out to be presented.*

## The Church is about to Change

When you have no governing, you have freedom in the Spirit that leads to chaos. I will lead the steps for The Rock of the Harbor church. The most holy early church environment was changed from the first century to the present time to look more and more like man's sinful nature, rather than my holy sanctuary. That is about to change! Study the church of Ephesus and learn about what went wrong. Grow in understanding because the time is here for the supernatural equipping of the saints. My Spirit will pour out rivers of revival and restoration. Delegate and allow people to mature in me.

## Jesus is Perfect Theology

I have already said that I see the outcome, and you have done very well to fulfill my best for you. Continue in obedience and I will continue in favor; be likened unto my son, Jesus—**He is perfect theology!** A seed must first die to produce life—so it is with you. I am teaching you to die to self daily. This is what you are learning:

Surrender leads to victory, and

Sacrifice leads to break-through transformation.

Serve me by serving others;

Bless me by blessing others;

Build the model of Church my way by my Spirit, and

Build the walls with love, mercy, kindness, and joy.

Be my representation of the fullness.

## Build the Model

Building the model means more than having a detailed plan on the how to—it is being responsible to oversee and boldly making adjustments when it is not as I have intended. The model will need to be properly maintained or it will attempt to change shape. You must know that the Destroyer has been very effective in changing my design. Like a thief of fine art who steals a painting in stages—stroke by stroke, the original masterpiece looks completely different when it is painted over.

## The Present Condition of the Church

- Testimonies, instead of being governed, have been eliminated;

- True fellowship has been destroyed by the quest for power and significance;

- Unity has been destroyed by pride masked by knowledge from education;

- Works have taken the place of grace;

- Selfishness has become increased above selflessness;

- Surrender, sacrifice, and submission have been made an alien; and

- Giving has been made to gain or profit.

My Church has opened the gates and welcomed the moneychangers. Gossip has been allowed to run rampant in the name of prayer needs and judgment. True repentance has been dampened by the wounds of condemnation. Many people don't feel safe in the Church anymore so they simply don't go. This is going to change!

## Adjustments Are Needed in My Church

- I want my Church repaired;

- I want healing and deliverance;

- I want love and mercy;

- I want Spirit-led, apostolic training;

- I want testimony that builds faith and gives glory;

- I want Spirit-filled worship—*NOT* self-exaltation;

- I want example-driven leadership, *NOT* hypocrisy; and

- I want real sacrifice, *NOT* illusion.

These are a few areas that need adjusting, and when this happens, there will be an outpouring of my Spirit that continues to increase, and those who attempt to duplicate this system will need divine direction, not just intelligence and resources. An apostolic movement of my Holy

Spirit cannot be done apart from my will—even with all the right ingredients.

I am the glue that binds together the substance:

- Faith without faithfulness is no faith at all;

- Process without prosperous divinity is weakness;

- Music without meaning is wasted attention; and

- Trying to become like the world to reach the world is compromise.

Become more Christ-like every day and you will reach the lost. Have fun. Keep the faith, and be on guard for the kingdom of Heaven is at hand, and the hand cannot contain it. All creation has reflected the divine nature of the expanse of my design. Follow my order and prosper.

# August 27th

## God Encourages a Faithful Pastor

*This prophetic word, given to my mother for a servant of God, shows to what extent the Lord understands what we are facing and his willingness to bring to light his purpose through it.*

My son, you are troubled about many things, but I am in the trouble. I am your God and you are my child, and I will never leave you nor forsake you. I will be with you through every difficult situation, which is part of my refining process. Clearing away the dross is not the fun part, but I say that the expectation of what the final product will become should give you cause to rejoice.

Your God is a refining fire.

> *"The refining pot is for silver and the furnace for gold, but the LORD tests the hearts."* (Proverbs 17:3)

I will turn up the heat on my Church at large, which includes your little flock—a flock that will have influence around the globe. Don't be discouraged, for you are purposefully and strategically placed. Growth will be coming to this area, and you will be involved in meeting the needs of the region. Your influence will surpass the borders of your congregation, for you have been faithful in little, and I will make you faithful in much.

*"And he said to him, 'Well done, good servant; because you were faithful in a very little, have authority over ten cities.'"* (Luke 19:17)

You have been wrongly judged by those who have not been given the right to judge.

*"Judge not, and you shall not be judged. Condemn not, and you shall not be condemned. Forgive, and you will be forgiven."* (Luke 6:37)

*"Indeed, let God be true but every man a liar. As it is written: "That you may be justified in Your words, and may overcome when You are judged."* (Romans 3:4)

They have usurped my authority and I am not pleased. I am your defender. Keep your mind stayed on me and I will give you rest. No weapon formed against you shall prosper or stand.

*"No weapon formed against you shall prosper and every tongue which rises against you in judgment you shall condemn. This is the heritage of the servants of the LORD, and their righteousness is from me," says the LORD."* (Isaiah 54:17)

I have seen your diligence; I have heard your many prayers given to me in secret, and I will reward you openly.

*"But you, when you pray, go into your room, and when you have shut your door, pray to your Father who is in the secret place; and your Father who sees in secret will reward you openly."* (Matthew 6:6)

I will give you the desires of your heart and will bless you beyond measure.

There will be more difficult times ahead, but I will give you wisdom and discernment to meet each challenge. If I laid out my plans, you would be overwhelmed, so I ask you to trust me as you seek me in the morning hours.

*"I rise before the dawning of the morning, and cry for help; I hope in your word."* (Psalm 119:147)

As you move through the events of your days, trust that what you do is part of the whole which will bring my kingdom back to earth. My bride needs adjustment before she is presented spotless, and I will guide you in making those adjustments. Do not fear what man can do to you or what man thinks of you, for you are my blood-bought son in whom I am well pleased.

*"The LORD is on my side; I will not fear. What can man do to me?"* (Psalm 118:6)

*"So we may boldly say: "The LORD is my helper; I will not fear. What can man do to me?"* (Hebrews 13:6)

I delight in you as you delight in your own sons. I am doing a work in each one of them in keeping with their individual nature or bent. They will burst through the limiting walls of the church to expand my kingdom in various ways, for I have placed my creative force in each one. Celebrate their differences, and rejoice as you see their manhood emerge.

September 2011

## September 2nd

**Kingdom Awareness**

I have shown you much about your present and your future. Not everyone is wired to house great capacities of kingdom awareness, but you will ride my wave of premium planetariums until you complete my pontification. Then its break will be pleasing to the patient and lovely to the lifeless. Break out of all your limiting mindsets, and set new expectations for heights and depths determined by my fashions and sanctions. Each step of faith I celebrate with great authority to reward diligent motion.

**The Prize of Hope**

Believe and move ever steadily toward the prize of hope.

> *"Behold, the eye of the LORD is on those who fear him, on those who hope in his mercy."* (Psalm 33:18)

You are just starting to see into the supernatural. You will not even recognize the faintness of what you now see in comparison to what I will show you.

*"For now we see in a mirror, dimly, but then face to face. Now I know in part, but then I shall know just as I also am known."* (1 Corinthians 13:12)

Lacking nothing begins with accepting that I have given you everything. I teach you now for the sole purpose of alignment and the pleasure of enjoying what I have purchased. Remember me when your success increases, and know that your praises will not cease but increase with the same measure.

# September 3rd

**Victory**

I, the Lord your God, am marching around the perimeter:

Cleansing,

Redeeming, and

Sanctifying.

Remember the Alamo! Pride comes before a fall. Victory is released into the hands of humility. Remember the victory? Vengeance is mine, and the victory is won so we battle from victory. Every eye has lain upon the truth, and the response has determined the individual battle's end. People need to outgrow their unbelief and believe fully and completely, maintaining faith to see the absolute victory.

> *"Now he did not do many mighty works there because of their unbelief."* (Matthew 13:58)

> *"Later he appeared to the eleven as they sat at the table; and he rebuked their unbelief and hardness of heart, because they did not believe those who had seen him after he had risen."* (Mark 16:14)

Victory is a battle of the mind, overcome in the thoughts where the seeds live. Some cultivate and tend to the weeds that choke out my beautiful blossoms of hope, life, and joy. Tend to your garden and plant goodness and mercy, and surely, they will be with you all of your days.

> *"Surely goodness and mercy shall follow me all the days of my life; and I will dwell in the house of the LORD forever."* (Psalm 23:6)

Great victory is found in the hardest trials, and

The hardest trials are allowed to bring unquenchable faith, and

Faith brings the substance of things hoped for.

> *"Now faith is the substance of things hoped for, the evidence of things not seen."* (Hebrews 11:1)

Do you battle differently when you know you have the victory? Yes. Confidence, calm assurance, and the readied sword of truth—swinging from faith, are powerful, and victorious against the Fowler's snare. Peace consumes your garden; goodness sends the daisies dancing—

Beautiful,

Plentiful,

Peaceful, and

Patient.

# September 4th

## The Rock

When you sit with me and sacrifice your time, I am well pleased. Many people whom I send to you will need gentle care because they are fragile and wounded. Keep in mind that I am sending the increase as I have promised. Don't be discouraged—much good is resulting at The Rock of the Harbor. Victory is my theme for this Sunday. Thank you for preparing.

## Instruction in Purity

Well done yesterday—you were victorious. I answered prayer. You cannot sleep now [it's 3:33 a.m.] because I longed to commune with you. I sit with you now for the purpose of instruction.

Prepare my pouring, and

Prosper with the Prince of Peace.

People pause and plunder

But as a plumber, I bring the plunger.

There's an easy way to avoid a backup and a simple way to keep things moving—it is:

Surrender,

   Sacrifice,

      Servant hood, and

         Sanctification.

It is selfless sowing and soundly seeding. I want my people pure as I myself am pure. Purity is not born from self-righteous piety, but from King-exalting loyalty.

*"Now the purpose of the commandment is love from a pure heart, from a good conscience, and from sincere faith."* (1 Timothy 1:5)

## Songs of the Spirit

Sing your songs this Sunday and let my Spirit fall on those who join your chorus. It is the anthem of heaven that leads the choir of angels.

My peace is the melody,

   My grace is the victory,

      My will is the song, and

         My life is the home.

Live in me that your supply will never end. As I increase your capacity, so others around you will be increased. I have brought duplication—not from duty but from dependence. Look for people to love and they will become your increase. Lift my name, Jesus, and the Savior will sanctify. Savor the sounds of salvation and settle your soul. I increase your ability to receive wisdom, and I increase your capacity to love and bless.

## Take a Walk with Me in the Spirit

Take a walk with me in the Spirit. Shut your eyes.

*Jesus appears and takes me to a beautiful beach with tan sand and he runs ahead and prepares for me a padded chair, a place to sit. He hands me a cold drink and puts on my head a rimmed hat to shade my eyes from his brightness. Then he draws instructions in the sand.*

When I send you—go; when I call you—come; when I ask you to—rest.

*He tries to pin an award on me, but there is no shirt to pin it on—only skin. He says,*

Don't look for any recognition.

*He draws a circle around me in the sand and says,*

Stay outside your comfort zone—it is where the faith is.

*Then he jacks up my seat as if to say,*

Your faith changes your perspective and your position.

*Now I find myself high above the beach, looking down at the tiny circle that was drawn around my chair, and he says,*

The mark is always where I am standing—don't miss it. Just keep your eyes on me—always just look to me: not the waves around you that crash upon the rock; not the grains of sand (minutia) and the monster mountains—just on me.

I am your supply;

   I am your every need;

      I am your present, and

         I am your sanctuary.

*I hear the song, "Sanctuary—Lord, prepare me to be a sanctuary, pure and holy, tried and true."*

There is more to life than living—

   There is more to do than is being done;

      There is farther to go.

There is a fountain that is flowing

   Far beyond the fruit tree after they have drunk.

      The fountain still supplies—

It is in the foggy forest that freedom cannot hide;

   It is in the treasure of temples

      That no man can divide.

*He then takes my hand and we walk down the beach together. He stops, gets down on all fours, and helps me stand up on his back. When I do, he changes into a ROCK. Standing on this rock, I see water pouring from it and draining into the ocean—fresh water and salt water. Animals of all kinds come and drink from the steam of fresh water and from the salt water. The ones who drink from the salt water fall and die and the ones who drink from the living water become refreshed and energized.*

My will is that everyone drinks from my well.

*"Then the woman of Samaria said to him, 'How is it that you, being a Jew, ask a drink from me, a Samaritan woman?' For Jews have no dealings with Samaritans. Jesus answered and said to her, 'If you knew the gift of God, and who it is who says to you, 'Give me a drink,' you would have asked him, and he would have given you living water.' The woman said to him, 'Sir, you have nothing to draw with, and the well is deep. Where then do you get that living water?'"* (John 4:9-11)

*"He who believes in me, as the Scripture has said, out of his heart will flow rivers of living water."* (John 7:38)

# September 5th

## God Gives me a Word to a Doctor

I have placed you in the center of the greatest need. My passion to heal the helpless has been carried through you. You will educate through the Church and the home church where the people are and where regulations and restrictions cannot tame the fire I've placed in you for justice. Let the naysayers motivate you and set your course toward victory. I will bring more doctors with the same passion to liberate the unsuspecting captives, and in me, you will succeed against all odds.

Add to your team of duplication. I will connect you to people with political influence and open doors. The foundation has been laid. I want the sick trained on wellness. Pour out your heart to educate; expose the darkness and you will build a network of liberators. All of your education was preparation for this present day. You need to gather the intercessors and surround yourself with prayers that my hand will move and mighty will it be.

You are on course, and all your work is coming to fruition. The seeds sown have been watered, and the waves of awareness travel beyond your direct appointments. I want you to prepare a DVD training series that will provide resources to fund the cause of information transformation. I am with you so who can be against you. I am supernaturally protecting what I have prepared to reveal; I will show you the way; I will open the doors.

## Harmony

Getting the most out of life means perfect harmony:

Heart,

  Soul,

    Mind, and

      Body.

I prepared the doctors to come and educate you on health. The government healthcare plan is smoke and mirrors—an illusion. America has been in the dark as a whole. Learn as much as you can on how to put the right things into your body and you will have a much better mindset and increased focus and clarity. I will use these doctors and they will be a part of my plan to free the captives of a medicated society. I will light a fire in each of them, and The Rock of the Harbor will be a launching pad for freeing the prisoners of ignorance.

## Random Instructions and Wisdoms

- Say only what I tell you to say and not a word that I don't.

- Be prepared just to love and love will cut through the dark like a sharp knife through butter.

- Let my peace become your peace, and then let it fall and blanket the torment.

- Stifle the mouth of the deceiver by loving outrageously. Those who cannot receive it are bound. Bless them and be gentle and gracious and I will drive the destroyers from their camp.

- Unity is the result of the absence of pride. Pride is the result of self.

- Servant hood, sacrifice, selflessness, surrender, submission, and sanctification are my accessories. Take them from my table and put them to work as the tools for feasting. My table is built on my promises and I keep every one.

*"For all the promises of God in him are yes, and in him Amen, to the glory of God through us."* (2 Corinthians 1:20)

Now eat and enjoy the fruit of my bounty: love, joy, peace, longsuffering, kindness, goodness, faithfulness, gentleness, and self-control.

*"But the fruit of the Spirit is love, joy, peace, longsuffering, kindness, goodness, faithfulness, gentleness, self-control. Against such there is no law."* (Galatians 5:22-23)

Consume these and these will consume others. Pour out and I'll pour in. Ponder palace principles and prosper.

*"And it shall come to pass in the last days, says God, That I will pour out of my Spirit on all flesh; Your sons and your daughters shall prophesy, Your young men shall see visions, Your old men shall dream dreams."* (Acts 2:17)

Do not allow yourself to be distracted; focus on me and I will reveal my agenda.

In all things give thanks and become a star that shines from heaven's goodness.

> *"In everything give thanks; for this is the will of God in Christ Jesus for you."* (1 Thessalonians 5:18)

I am filling you with every needed assurance, and I have given you the ability to pull down strongholds and crush generational curses. Begin to call out the declarations of victory over my children and decree my covenants over them. I will cause it to be so.

> *"For the weapons of our warfare are not carnal but mighty in God for pulling down strongholds, casting down arguments and every high thing that exalts itself against the knowledge of God, bringing every thought into captivity to the obedience of Christ, and being ready to punish all disobedience when your obedience is fulfilled."* (2 Corinthians 10:4-6)

## I Am Moving You

Stretch yourself across my sandy beach and hear the roar of victory crashing upon the rough edges of you. I will smooth you into a gem of great value. Nothing can stop what I am designing. Do not run away from my course—not even in your mind. There is no turning back, and defeat is no longer an option. You are an outrageous force of motion because I myself am moving you.

## Discernment

No weapon formed against you will be rewarded but crushed as the head of every serpent rises to oppose you.

*"No weapon formed against you shall prosper, and every tongue which rises against you in judgment You shall condemn. This is the heritage of the servants of the LORD, and their righteousness is from me," says the LORD."* (Isaiah 54:17)

I give you now a heightened level of discernment to see into the grasses of darkness for what slithers beneath the surface. Be on guard and praise me—even for what is not yet seen, and it will come into focus as you press on.

## Numbers

I want you to remember: do not measure success by numbers; allow those who do to be deceived, and then I will pour out continually to bring the deep and the wide. Every life is valuable to me, and everyone wants to do great things for me. Just instruct them and point them to my direction. Help is on the way. Don't worry about your position—just move as I lead you, and remember that you will not stay in one place but will move around the country.

## Community Transformation

This is the quiet before the quakes, so don't be surprised by my stirring. Peace is pressing your assailers, and I will bring community transformation.

## Thank You

Thank you for giving me your time—these are my most precious moments. No one can stop what I have put in motion, not even you. Your willingness is an open door, and I will continue to flow through the door of your heart, so do not allow any bitterness to shut the door. Resentment will knock on the door of a shut heart, but let my love flow so abundantly through you that an open heart represents my pouring beyond all bitterness pressing against it. I will deal with everyone who speaks against you. I alone will be your defender. Get up and stand against the wind of my breath and breathe upon the breathless from rivers of life.

## The Prize

Focus on the prize, and

   Let the prize unwrap your lesson.

Give grace, and

   Grace will become your place of rest.

Mourn with those who mourn, and

   Joy will come in the morning.

Every effort you make toward victory

   Is an effort toward peace.

Victorious people have peace, and

   Peace is coveted by the restless rich.

Peace is the result of trusting, and

   Trusting comes from understanding;

Understanding is a result of reflection, and

   Reflection is a result of meditation.

Turn on my lamp, and

Let it shine upon your path,

Renewing your awareness and

Restoring your perceptions.

## Walk on the Soil of Your Mind

Do you know what I am preparing? You know what I have shown you. Gaze into my heart's prayer and cry with me. It is not my will that any should perish.

> *"The Lord is not slack concerning His promise, as some count slackness, but is longsuffering toward us, not willing that any should perish but that all should come to repentance."* (2 Peter 3:9)

Be present with me and absent from the body. Denying its cravings will produce much fruit that many can taste and see. Take my bounty to those who do not have, and let my focus become the neck that turns the head in the direction of the need.

> *"We are confident, yes, well pleased rather to be absent from the body and to be present with the Lord."* (2 Corinthians 5:8)

Serve my chosen leaders and give them your life for your life is found in losing it.

> *"He who finds his life will lose it, and he who loses his life for my sake will find it."* (Matthew 10:39)

Walk now on the soil of your mind where I have preserved the seed that comes forth to produce the full measure of imagination. Great is the reward to those, whose unwavering trust is in me,

For steady is the stream of everlasting, and

Constant is the roar of my blessing.

## I Move Mountains

Sitting with me activates all that I am releasing, and beyond your hopes, I move mountains. I'll tell you when to run, and you will move as the gazelle. When your eyes perceive what is on the horizon,

Dance, and

   Run, and

     Sing

So that rejoicing fills my house and cannot be contained.

## Open Your Windows

*In a vision, I pushed opened a shuttered window and looked out on a field that expanded as far as my eyes could see. It was filled with a myriad of flora and fauna, splashed with every color imaginable, and a variety of birds were flying about, chirping their birdsongs.*

Open your windows so all who hear can enjoy what I have sent out. My Holy Spirit goes forth with the pleasing aroma of a fresh spring-time blooming. Pick from this field and hand out the anointing, and I will expand it before it withers. Flowers picked cannot thrive unless they are given away and put to use for the enjoyment of many. To be enjoyed, every seed must die to self and then be broken before it brings forth life. Let me fill you with lessons as you gather the melodies of heaven. Add this one to your collection.

## Boldness of Faith

When you step out with boldness of faith and seek my fullness, I will reward you with boldness of action and you will surely receive my full measure. Consume all that I say, for it will be released from you like the sunrise of a new day. Don't think too hard. Your purpose in me is simple—you were fashioned by my purposes to carry out your destiny. The Fowler still tries to snatch you, but what stays in my hand cannot be taken from me. Stay in my hand in every thought and I will place you in the covering of my protection.

> *"My sheep hear my voice, and I know them, and they follow me. And I give them eternal life, and they shall never perish; neither shall anyone snatch them out of my hand. My Father, who has given them to me, is greater than all; and no one is able to snatch them out of my Father's hand."* (John 10:27-29)

This is the season for rain, and rain is what brings the harvest. I have said it will be astounding.

> *"For the earth which drinks in the rain that often comes upon it, and bears herbs useful for those by whom it is cultivated, receives blessing from God."* (Hebrews 6:7)

Rest in the reasons I desire to use you. I snatched you from death's dungeon and have firmly placed you upon the springboard of safety.

> *"He sets on high those who are lowly, and those who mourn are lifted to safety."* (Job 5:11)

## Live Out My Word

Life is not measured by living, but by living out every word that comes from my mouth.

> *"But He answered and said, "It is written, 'Man shall not live by bread alone, but by every word that proceeds from the mouth of God.'"* (Matthew 4:4)

Is not the blesser more important than the blessing? After all, if given the choice, would a child rather have a gumball or the machine that produced it? People seek my gifts, but they don't take the time to get to know the giver. I liken this to the dying, godless world, which has lost its way in the dark, guided by the dimmest form of selfishness.

## I Am the Lover of Your Soul

People look for direction but don't want a director. They sow discord and expect to reap peace and harmony. I say, love one another as yourself and raise the banner high that says, "I love the Lord with all my heart, soul, and strength."

> *"You shall love the Lord your God with all your heart, with all your soul, and with all your strength."* (Deuteronomy 6:5)

The way you treat your neighbor shows your love for me.

> *"You shall not take vengeance, nor bear any grudge against the children of your people, but you shall love your neighbor as yourself: I am the LORD."* (Leviticus 19:18)

> *"So he answered and said, "'You shall love the LORD your God with all your heart, with all your soul, with all your strength, and with all your mind,' and 'your neighbor as yourself.'"* (Luke 10:27)

Some speak as if they are trying to convince themselves. A lover is only as good as the object in which that love is placed. Things of this world are fleeting. I am the lover of your soul and have tended to your garden. The fence is for keeping people out. The gate is for those I let in. The nibbles of foxes spoil the vine, but encouragement steers a heart toward excellence.

## It's NOT Meant to Be a Secret

Book number one is ready for review. Allow me to highlight the words I have chosen for you to work with. *It's* NOT *Meant to Be a Secret— God wants to speak to you!:* All of these writings are a result of time with me, and spending time with me is what I long for every believer to do. How I long to gather them, but they do not come. Point them back, beloved—this is my heart's cry. It is not my will that my creation ignore me. Let this book share what was not meant to be a secret and I will whisper light to the darkness.

> *"O Jerusalem, Jerusalem, the one who kills the prophets and stones those who are sent to her! How often I wanted to gather your children together, as a hen gathers her chicks under her wings, but you were not willing!"* (Matthew 23:37)

# Addendum

*This word from the Lord was given recently to an Equipping Group at The Rock of the Harbor. When we sat together and followed the five steps listed below, many heard the voice of the Lord for the first time. Excitement filled the air as well as the Spirit of God. Many were healed of various infirmities as a result.*

## How to Hear My Voice

### *I Will Teach You*

I want you to teach others how to move in hearing my voice and how to exercise faith through prophecy. Prophecy is the result of hearing me, for I tell you things you do not know. You have heard it said, "Don't show people how big your fish is—teach them how to fish." I am telling you to show others how to hear, just like you yourself have been hearing.

### *Steps to Hearing*

1. Get quiet.

2. Communicate with God.

3. Expect to hear (getting your pen and paper ready is faith).

4. Write down what the Lord says.

5. Share with others as you are led.

### *Practicum*

Many Christians hear so many different things about hearing my voice, but the truth about hearing is this: I am a rewarder of those who diligently seek me.

> *"But without faith it is impossible to please him: for he that cometh to God must believe that he is, and that he is a rewarder of them that diligently seek him."* (Hebrews 11:6 KJV)

I am the one who surrounds surrender. Faith is the substance of believing you will hear. Not believing you will hear is why people don't.

> *"Now faith is the substance of things hoped for, the evidence of things not seen."* (Hebrews 11:1)

Say something like this: "He (Jesus) is here right now," or "Adjust your awareness of his presence." Where two or more are gathered together, there I am in the midst of them.

> *"For where two or three are gathered together in my name, I am there in the midst of them."* (Matthew 18:20)

Believe first and your faith will be fully manifest. Ask everyone to cry out to me, "Jesus, are you there?" or "You're here, aren't you, Jesus?" I am your built-in teacher!

> *"A disciple is not above his teacher, but everyone who is perfectly trained will be like his teacher."* (Luke 6:40)

## A Prayer to Receive Christ

Lord God, I know I am a sinner. I believe you sent your son, Jesus, to die on a cross for my sin. I repent of my wicked ways and ask you to come into my heart and fill me with your Holy Spirit. Cleanse me of all unrighteousness and I will live for you from this day on. I want you to be my Lord. Thank you. Amen.

## A Prayer of Release

Dear Lord: I purpose and choose to forgive (name) for (what he/she did) from my heart. I cancel all his/her debts and obligations to me—he/she owes me nothing! I ask you to forgive me for my bitterness and unforgiveness toward (name) in this situation. In the name of Jesus and by the power of his blood, I cancel Satan's authority over me in this memory because I have forgiven (name). I command all the tormentors assigned to me, because of my unforgiveness, to leave me, now. Holy Spirit, I invite you into my heart to heal me of this pain. Please speak your truth to me about this situation and I will listen for your answer.

## A Prayer of Forgiveness of Self

Dear heavenly Father, in the name of Jesus, and as an act of my own free will, I confess, repent, and renounce my (specific sin of self-loathing). I ask you to forgive me for this sin. I purpose and choose to forgive myself for (specific sin) from my heart. I release myself from any guilt and shame because of this self-bitterness. In the name of Jesus, and by the power of his blood, I cancel Satan's authority over me in this area because of my cooperation with self-bitterness. I command self-bitterness to go now. Holy Spirit, I invite you into my heart to heal me of self-bitterness. Please speak your words of truth to me about this situation and I will listen quietly.

# About the Author

Compelled by a passion to share what God has done in his life, Nathan A. French established Turn Around Ministries (www.TurnAroundMinistry.com), a non-profit organization, and has published two CD albums: Open My Heart and Turn Around. Nathan writes the lyrics as well as the supporting tunes and sings in a conversational, convicting style. All the songs are born out of personal experience and bear the marks of authenticity—marks of pain, struggle, redemption, submission, and triumph. He is the founder of The Rock of the Harbor equipping center, a church located in the heart of Gig Harbor, Washington (www.RockoftheHarbor.com). It's NOT Meant to Be a Secret, Nathan's first book, is a compilation of words given to him during his conversations with the Lord.

Made in the USA
Coppell, TX
07 March 2021

50782113R00207